William Sutherland

Constitutions of the R.W. Grand Lodge, Subordinate
and Rebekah Degree Lodges, I.O.O.F. of Nevada

ISBN/EAN: 9783337219697

Printed in Europe, USA, Canada, Australia, Japan

Cover: Foto ©ninafisch / pixelio.de

More available books at **www.hansebooks.com**

William Sutherland

Constitutions of the R.W. Grand Lodge, Subordinate

and Rebekah Degree Lodges, I.O.O.F. of Nevada

CONSTITUTIONS

R. W. GRAND LODGE,

Subordinate and Rebekah Degree Lodges,

I. O. O. F. OF NEVADA,

TOGETHER WITH

Code of Procedure Regulating Charges and Trials, Digest
of Decisions, and Standing Resolutions,

UP TO AND INCLUDING THE

FIFTEENTH ANNUAL COMMUNICATION,

1881.

VIRGINIA, NEVADA:

WM. SUTHERLAND, PRINTER, 23 SOUTH C STREET.

1881.

PROCEEDINGS

R. W. GRAND LODGE, I. O. O. F.,

OF NEVADA.

At the Fifteenth Annual Communication, held at Eureka
in June, A. D. 1881, the following action was had relative to the
printing of the Constitutions, etc. On the fourth day of the
session, to wit: on the 10th day of June, Rep. LAWS offered the
following resolutions (Journal, page 197), which were, on motion,
adopted:

Resolved, That the Grand Secretary is instructed to have the Revised Constitution of Subordinates, Constitution of Degree of Rebekah Lodges and Digest
of Decisions adopted by this R. W. Grand Lodge printed in pamphlet form,
separately from the Journal of Proceedings of this session, and that such Constitutions and Decisions be omitted from the Journal.

Resolved, further, That the Constitution of this R. W. Grand Lodge, Code regulating Trials annd Appeals, and Standing Resolutions be also printed in such pamphlet.

J. G. LAWS, of No. 14.

Subsequently, upon motion of Rep. BENCE, of No. 4 (page 202), six hundred copies of said pamphlet were ordered to be printed, for distribution to Lodges and Past Grands.

ATTEST:

WM. H. HILL,
Grand Secretary.

CONSTITUTION

OF THE

R. W. GRAND LODGE, I. O. O. F.,

OF THE

STATE OF NEVADA,

Up to the Fifteenth Annual Session, 1881.

WHEREAS, The Right Worthy Grand Lodge of the Independent Order of Odd Fellows, of the United States of America, now the Sovereign Grand Lodge, I. O. O. F., possessing original and exclusive jurisdiction—the source of all true and legitimate authority in Odd Fellowship throughout the world— did, by its warrant, bearing date the nineteenth day of September, 1866, in the forty-eighth year of our Order, grant authority to certain Past Grands of the Order, resident in the State of Nevada, to form a Grand Lodge of the Independent Order of Odd Fellows, to be known and hailed by the name, style and title of the Right Worthy Grand Lodge of the Independent Order of Odd Fellows of the State of Nevada, giving and granting to them and their successors, by the name, style and title aforesaid, full power and authority to grant warrants for opening Lodges subordinate to it, for the propagation of the established principles of the Order; with power and authority, also, to cause all honorary and the first three degrees of the Order to be conferred on deserving members, according to the laws, customs and ancient usages of the Independent Order of Odd Fellows; and as the Grand Legislative Head of the Order in the State of Nevada, to have and to exercise full power and authority to enforce upon its subordinates a strict adherence to the laws of the Order, and to make and establish such rules for the government as in the opinion of said Grand Lodge may be for the advancement of the Order, and in conformity of the direction of the Sovereign Grand Lodge, I. O. O. F.

Now, therefore, we, the Past Grands, residing within said jurisdiction, do hereby make and declare the following as the Constitution of the R. W. Grand Lodge of the Independent Order of Odd Fellows, for the State of Nevada:

ARTICLE I.

NAME.

This Grand Lodge shall be known by the name, style and title of the "Right Worthy Grand Lodge of the Independent Order of Odd Fellows of the State of Nevada."

ARTICLE II.

POWER OF THE GRAND LODGE.

This Grand Lodge, within the limitations imposed by its Charter and the Constitution and Laws of the Sovereign Grand Lodge, I. O. O. F., possesses within the State of Nevada supreme legislative, executive and judicial authority. It has the right and power to grant dispensations to establish Lodges, to charter Lodges, to provide Constitutions for the government of the same, to suspend or discontinue for any cause any Lodge subordinate to it, to hear and determine all appeals from the decisions and acts of its Subordinate Lodges and from the decisions of the M. W. Grand Master, to redress grievances of Lodges or members under its jurisdiction, to punish by reprimand, fine or expulsion from its body any of its members, or any of the Past Grands present at any of its sessions, who shall refuse to obey its laws or who shall be guilty of conduct unbecoming an Odd Fellow, and to do whatever is proper according to the usages of Odd Fellowship not inconsistent with the provisions of this Constitution or the Constitution and Laws of the Sovereign Grand Lodge, I. O. O. F. No Lodge of this Order shall exist in this State without the permission of this Grand Lodge.

ARTICLE III.

MEMBERSHIP.

SECTION 1. This Grand Lodge shall be composed of its elective officers, Representatives elected as hereinafter provided, and Past Grand Masters (as Representatives of the jurisdiction at large). All Past Grands of this jurisdiction in good standing in their respective Lodges, and possessed of the Grand Lodge Degree, may be present at the sessions of the Grand Lodge, but shall not be entitled to vote, except as provided in this Constitution; and shall not be entitled to speak upon any subject without permission.

SEC. 2. Every Lodge shall be entitled in the Grand Lodge to three Representatives for its Charter, and one Representative for every fifteen members in good standing. Representatives must be Past Grands in good standing, and shall be elected by the Lodge at any regular meeting within two months previous to each Annual Communication, to serve one year from the beginning of said Annual Communication. Vacancies may be filled at any time—by election by the Lodge—to serve the remainder of the term, and all Past Grand Masters of this jurisdiction, in good standing in their respective Lodges, shall be entitled to the same privileges as Representatives.

SEC. 3. Before a Representative or other Past Grand can take his seat in this Grand Lodge he must have received the Grand Lodge Degree.

ARTICLE IV.

VOTING.

SECTION 1. Each elective officer, except the M. W. Grand Master, who is not also a Representative, and each Representative shall be entitled to one vote. In the temporary absence of any Representative, the Representatives of the Lodge present may cast the vote of the absentee. The Most Worthy Grand Master shall give the casting vote whenever the Grand Lodge is equally divided, except in cases of election of officers. In the election of Grand Officers each Past Grand in attendance at the Annual Communication shall be entitled to one vote only.

SEC. 2. All voting in this Grand Lodge, except as hereinafter specified, shall be *viva voce*, and all questions shall be determined by a majority of the votes given. Upon a call therefor by five (5) members, the yeas and nays shall be taken and recorded upon the Journal. The yeas and nays shall also be taken when required by this Constitution.

SEC. 3. In the election of officers of this Grand Lodge the vote shall be by ballot; each officer shall be voted for separately, and a majority of the valid votes cast (a quorum voting) shall be necessary to a choice.

ARTICLE V.

SESSIONS.

SECTION 1. The Grand Lodge shall hold regular Annual Communications, to begin on the first Tuesday after the first Monday in June of each year, at 10 o'clock A. M., and continue from day to day, upon its own adjournment, until the business of the session is disposed of.

Sec. 2. Special sessions shall be called for the transaction of extraordinary business by the M. W. Grand Master on application, by resolution under seal, of a majority of Lodges. No other business shall be transacted than that specified in the call, and not less than thirty days' notice shall be given, by letter, under seal of the Grand Lodge and attested by the Grand Secretary, to each Representative, which thirty days shall begin from the date on which said letters are mailed. Such special sessions shall be held at the place of meeting of the last annual ression.

Sec. 3. Special sessions may also be called by the Grand Master, at such times and places as he may determine, to instruct in the unwritten work and to confer the Past Official and Grand Lodge Degrees, at which session must be present the Grand Master, the Deputy Grand Master or the Grand Warden, and the Grand Secretary and five Past Grands in good standing, and no other business shall be transacted than is provided for in this section.

Sec. 4. The Grand Lodge cannot be opened at any regular or special session, except as provided for instruction in the work and degrees, unless Representatives from twelve Lodges are present.

ARTICLE VI.

OFFICERS, AND THEIR ELECTION.

Section 1. The officers of this Grand Lodge shall be: Most Worthy Grand Master, Right Worthy Deputy Grand Master, Right Worthy Grand Warden, Right Worthy Grand Secretary, Right Worthy Grand Treasurer, and two Right Worthy Grand Representatives to the Sovereign Grand Lodge, I. O. O. F., all of whom shall be elected by ballot; Worthy Grand Chaplain, Worthy Grand Marshal, Worthy Grand Conductor, Worthy Grand Guardian, Worthy Grand Herald, and District Deputy Grand Master for each District, all of whom shall be appointed by the Grand Master and approved by the Grand Lodge.

Sec. 2. The elective officers of this Grand Lodge shall be chosen by ballot at 1 o'clock P. M., on the third day of the session, at which time each Past Grand present shall be entitled to place candidates in nomination for the respective offices. The Grand Master shall appoint two tellers, who shall receive the ballots of those persons entitled to vote in a box provided for that purpose; and when all have voted who wish, the Grand Master shall declare the ballot closed, whereupon the tellers shall proceed to canvass the vote. Should there be no choice, the Grand Master shall immediately order another ballot; should there be no choice upon the second ballot, another ballot shall be ordered. The Past Grand receiving the majority of all the votes cast (a quorum voting) shall be declared by the Grand Master elected, and on the last day of the session shall be installed in his office; *provided*, that an officer elect may be installed at any time, upon a four-fifths' vote of the Lodge affirmatively, but the officer so installed shall not assume the duties of the office until the last day of the session.

SEC. 3. No Past Grand shall be eligible for any elective office, except Grand Representatives, unless he is a member of the Grand Lodge and present at the session, and has attained such degrees as by virtue of his office he may confer upon others.

SEC. 4. Vacancies in the office of District Deputy Grand Master shall be filled by the Grand Master; vacancies in the other Grand offices, except that of Grand Master, shall be filled by the Grand Lodge, if in session; if not, then by the Executive Committee, for the remainder of the term.

ARTICLE VII.

DUTIES OF OFFICERS.

SECTION 1. The Most Worthy Grand Master shall preside at all sessions of the Grand Lodge, and preserve order therein, enforce the laws of the Sovereign Grand Lodge, I. O. O. F., and the Constitution, Laws and Rules of this R. W. Grand Lodge; decide all questions of order and law, and enforce the same, subject to an appeal to the Grand Lodge. He shall appoint all Grand Officers pro tem., and all committees not otherwise provided for in the Constitution or ordered by the Grand Lodge. He shall give the casting vote in all cases where the votes are equally divided, except in cases of election of officers. When any demand shall have been approved by a majority of the Finance Committee, he shall order the Grand Treasurer to pay the same. He may grant dispensations on the application of a Lodge to confer the degrees on a member without delay. He may in person confer the Past Official Degrees. He shall decide all appeals on questions of law which may be made to him from the decisions of District Deputies, which decision shall be binding until reversed by the Grand Lodge. He shall receive and act on all complaints that may be made to him of the acts of District Deputies or Lodges. He shall give such instructions from time to time in the work of the Order to the Deputies or the Lodges as may be necessary, and at each Annual Communication of the Grand Lodge shall report all acts that he may have done in accordance with the authority conferred upon him. All powers pertaining to this Grand Lodge not specifically mentioned in this Constitution as being conferred on the Grand Master, are, unless delegated by the Grand Lodge, expressly withheld.

SEC. 2. The Right Worthy Deputy Grand Master shall support the Most Worthy Grand Master in the Grand Lodge, and shall be invested with his powers during his temporary absence, and in the event of a vacancy in the office of Grand Master, the Deputy Grand Master shall become Grand Master for the remainder of the term, and receive the honors of a full term.

2

SEC. 3: The Right Worthy Grand Warden shall assist the Grand Master in conducting the business of the Grand Lodge. He shall by direction of the Grand Master confer the Past Official and Grand Lodge Degrees during the session of the Grand Lodge on all that are qualified to receive them. By direction of the Grand Master, he shall have special charge of the door, and in the absence of the Grand Master and Deputy Grand Master he shall preside.

SEC. 4. The Right Worthy Grand Secretary shall attend every meeting of the Grand Lodge with the books and papers of the Lodge. He shall keep a correct record of the proceedings of the Grand Lodge at every session, and transmit, as soon as practicable after the close of the annual session, two copies thereof to each subordinate Lodge in the jurisdiction. He shall keep the accounts between the Grand Lodge and its subordinates, collect all moneys due the Grand Lodge and pay the same immediately to the Grand Treasurer. He shall issue all necessary notices and circulars to subordinates, Representatives and Officers. He shall attest and affix the seal of the Grand Lodge to all proclamations, dispensations and circulars of the Grand Master to Subordinate Lodges, and keep a record of the same; conduct the correspondence of the Grand Lodge, receive all documents relative to the Grand Lodge and make proper disposition of them; provide all stationery for the use of the Grand Lodge and its officers; superintend such printing as the Lodge shall direct, and perform such other duties as properly pertain to his office, or may be directed by the Grand Lodge. He shall receive such salary, payable quarterly, as may be fixed upon at each annual session of the Lodge. He shall, previous to installation, give bonds to the Grand Lodge in such form and penalty as may be approved of, for the faithful discharge of his duties.

SEC. 5. The Right Worthy Grand Treasurer shall receive and take charge of the moneys of the Grand Lodge; pay all orders drawn on him by the Grand Master and countersigned by the Grand Secretary, under the seal of the Grand Lodge; make such investment of the funds as the Grand Lodge may direct; keep his accounts in such manner as will exhibit the source and amount of receipts; the purpose and amount of disbursements, and to whom paid; have his accounts closed up on the day previous to the meeting of the Grand Lodge, annually, and submit them to the Finance Committee, and transmit through the Grand Secretary annually to the Grand Lodge an exhibit of his accounts. He shall attend all regular sessions of the Grand Lodge, and shall, previous to installation, give bonds to the Grand Lodge, in such form and penalty as shall be approved of, for the faithful performance of his duties.

SEC. 6. The District Deputy Grand Master, shall, in the absence of the Grand Master, install the officers of all Lodges in his District; enforce observance of the Constitution, By-Laws and Resolutions of the Grand Lodge and the Constitution of the Subordinate Lodges; be the organ of the Grand Master with the subordinates in his district; have power to grant dispensations to

Lodges in his district to confer the degrees in less time than may be otherwise permitted, when circumstances require it. He shall see that the work of the Order is performed uniformly in such manner as he may have been instructed by the Grand Master; confer Past Official Degrees, collect from Lodges in his district all returns and moneys due the Grand Lodge, and forward them immediately to the Grand Secretary; decide all questions of law that may be submitted to him by Lodges under his charge, and report semi-annually to the Grand Master all his official acts. He shall forthwith report to the Grand Master all cases of violation, on the part of subordinates, of the Constitution and By-laws of the Grand Lodge, disobedience to its lawful commands, or violation of the Constitution of Subordinates.

SEC. 7. The appointed officers of this Grand Lodge, whose duties are not hereinbefore defined, shall perform such duties as are required by their charges and the usages of the Order.

SEC. 8. There shall be elected annually three Trustees of this R. W. Grand Lodge, whose duty it shall be to hold in trust for the R. W. Grand Lodge all stocks, securities, investments, properties and funds belonging to the Grand Lodge, and to transfer, exchange or deposit the same, or any part thereof, when required by the Grand Lodge so to do. It shall be their duty to draw from the Treasurer, by draft regularly drawn, such sums of money as the Grand Lodge may direct, and invest the same for the best interests of the Grand Lodge, in such way as it may approve; to collect interest regularly when due, and pay the same over to the Grand Lodge; to call in loans, or sue for the same, whenever the Grand Lodge requires them so to do. The Grand Lodge may require them to give good and sufficient bonds, and fix the amount, for the faithful performance of their duties. They shall have power to transact the necessary business for the comfort and convenience of the Grand Lodge, and at the expiration of one year make their annual report.

ARTICLE VIII.
OFFENSES AND PUNISHMENTS.

SECTION 1. Any Grand Officer may be removed from his office, by the Grand Lodge, for misconduct or neglect of duty, but he shall be entitled to a fair trial, and two-thirds of the votes of the Representatives present, affirmatively, shall be necessary for removal.

SEC. 2. No officer shall officiate in the Grand Lodge during the time of his trial. Whenever the Grand Master, or officer acting as such, shall be on trial, or whenever a resolution for the removal of the Grand Master, or officer acting as such, shall be submitted, the Grand Lodge may direct any Past Grand Master—in case the Deputy Grand Master and Grand Warden are incapacitated—to occupy the chair.

SEC. 3. Any member or Past Grand may be fined, reprimanded or ex-pelled from the Grand Lodge, as such, for misconduct, upon a fair trial, and the vote of two-thirds of the members present at any meeting.

ARTICLE IX.

COMMITTEES.

SECTION 1. The elective Grand Officers, except the Grand Representa-tives, shall constitute the Executive Committee, to act in the recess of the annual session of the Grand Lodge, and perform such duties as shall be referred to it. The Grand Master shall be Chairman of said Committee, and he may call meetings thereof at his discretion.

SEC. 2. The Most Worthy Grand Master shall, at each annual session, immediately after the installation of the Grand Officers, appoint the following Standing Committees : (1) on Credentials, three members; (2) on Finance, three members; (3) on State of the Order, five members; (4) on Legislation, five members; (5) on Appeals, five members; (6) on Laws of Subordinates, three members; (7) on Petitions, five members; (8) on Rebekah Degree, five members.

SEC. 3. The Committee on Credentials shall examine and report without delay to the Grand Lodge on the credentials and certificates of Representa-tives and Past Grands.

SEC. 4. The Committee on Finance shall report upon all accounts and claims against the Grand Lodge, previous to such accounts being allowed; it shall examine annually the accounts of the R. W. Grand Secretary and R. W. Grand Treasurer, and report the result of the examination and the condition of the finances immediately thereafter to the Grand Lodge; it shall audit the accounts of all officers and committees entrusted with the receipt and disburse-ment of funds of the Grand Lodge; it shall report at each annual session the amount required for the expenses of the Grand Lodge for the ensuing year, and suggest such measures of finance as it may deem expedient.

SEC. 5. The Committee on the State of the Order shall report upon the reports of the Most Worthy Grand Master and Right Worthy Grand Secretary, in so far as they relate to the state of the Order; it shall examine the reports of the District Deputy Grand Masters, and such other matter as may be referred to it, and report thereon to the Grand Lodge. The Committee shall also report upon the condition and progress of the Order in this jurisdiction, and recom-mend such measures for the good of the Order as it from time to time shall deem proper.

SEC. 6. The Committee on Legislation shall report on all resolutions referred to it proposing amendments to the Constitution, the enactment, amendment or repeal of any law, by-law, rule of order or resolution governing the Grand Lodge, and upon such other matters as may be referred to it.

SEC. 7. The Committee on Appeals shall examine all appeals referred to it, and report thereon to the Grand Lodge. All appeals taken from the action of subordinate Lodges shall, as soon as they are received by the Grand Secretary, be transmitted by him to the Chairman of the Committee on Appeals; if the committee finds the papers defective in any essential particular it shall certify the fact to the Grand Secretary, returning the papers to him, who shall transmit them to the Subordinate Lodge, requiring it forthwith to correct the defects complained of, and return the amended papers immediately through the Grand Secretary to the Chairman of the Committee on Appeals. It shall be the duty of the Committee on Appeals to report on the earliest practicable day of the annual session its action upon the appeals transmitted to it during the recess of the Grand Lodge.

SEC. 8. The Committee on Laws of Subordinates shall examine the by-laws of subordinates, and, when in accordance with the laws of this jurisdiction and the usages of the Order, approve them, and when said by-laws are in conflict with the laws of this jurisdiction and the usages of the Order, it shall disapprove of them and return them to the Lodge with the objections thereto.

SEC. 9. The Committee on Petitions shall examine all petitions referred to it and report to the Grand Lodge such action thereon as may be proper.

SEC. 10. The Committee on the Rebekah Degree shall examine and report on all matters pertaining to the Rebekah Degree and Rebekah Degree Lodges that may be referred to it.

ARTICLE X.

REVENUE.

SECTION 1. The revenue of the Grand Lodge shall be raised and used for the purpose of paying the necessary expenses thereof, and for no other purpose.

SEC. 2. Every Subordinate Lodge shall pay to the Grand Lodge such capitation tax as may from year to year be determined upon, assessed upon the active members of the Lodge, as may appear upon the report of December 31st preceding the annual session of the Grand Lodge, the amount of said assessment to be determined by the Finance Committee, after having ascertained what probable sum will be necessary to pay the expenses of the Grand Lodge for the current year, the assessment so levied to be paid to the District Deputy Grand Master, and by him transmitted to the Grand Secretary, semi-annually in January and July.

Sec. 3. No Lodge under the jurisdiction of this Grand Lodge shall be entitled to have its officers installed or to receive the traveling or term P. W. until the prescribed reports to the Grand Lodge and all moneys due the same shall have been placed in the hands of the installing officer.

ARTICLE XI.

CHARTERS OF SUBORDINATES.

Section 1. Charters may be granted as follows: On the written application of five or more Brothers of the Order, one of whom has attained the Scarlet Degree, praying for a charter to open a Lodge where there is no Lodge established; on the application of seven or more Brothers, five of whom must be of the Scarlet Degree, for a charter to open a Lodge where there is one already established; *provided*, that the nearest Subordinate Lodge in the district shall recommend that such charter be granted. All applications for charters must be accompanied by the withdrawal cards or dismissal certificates, and by the charter fee, to-wit, thirty dollars; should the Grand Lodge not be in session, application for a charter may be made to the Executive Committee, through the Grand Secretary, which shall have power to issue a dispensation, if deemed advisable, to open such Lodge, subject to confirmation by the Grand Lodge at its next annual session.

Sec. 2. Every Lodge opened in this jurisdiction shall be instituted by the Most Worthy Grand Master, District Deputy Grand Master or by a Past Grand especially deputed, who shall give to the Lodge, with the charter, the necessary instructions and charges. The expenses of the instituting officer shall be paid by the Lodge instituted.

Sec. 3. On the written petition of one or more Past Grands, and four or more Scarlet Degree Brothers of the Order, all of whom shall be in good standing and in possession of the Degree of Rebekah, and five or more Daughters of Rebekah, praying for a charter to open a Rebekah Degree Lodge, the Grand Lodge may grant the same, and such Degree Lodge shall receive its charter and the necessary lectures and instructions in the same manner as is provided for Subordinate Lodges.

Sec. 4. On the written petition of three or more Subordinate Lodges embraced in one district praying for a warrant to open a Degree Lodge, the Grand Lodge may grant the same; and such Degree Lodge shall receive its charter and the necessary lectures and instructions in the same manner as is provided for Subordinate Lodges.

Sec. 5. No Degree Lodge shall admit or retain in membership any person who is not a member in good standing of a Subordinate Lodge within the district.

ARTICLE XII.

REPORTS OP SUBORDINATES.

SECTION 1. At the end of each term every Subordinate Lodge shall report to the Grand Lodge the work thereof for such term, which shall include the names of those initiated, admitted by card as Ancient Odd Fellows, rejected, withdrawn by card, reinstated and deceased; the names of those suspended and ' expelled and the cause thereof; also, of those dropped from membership, together with the number of degrees conferred, the whole number in membership, the amount of receipts and disbursements, and the result of the election of officers, accompanied by whatever amount may be due the Grand Lodge. On the 31st day of December of each year every Lodge shall report to the Grand Lodge a full return of members, with their names ranked according to the degrees they have taken, and a statement of the number of Brothers relieved, widowed families relieved, Brothers buried, orphans educated, and the amount of money expended for each of these purposes.

ARTICLE XIII.

OFFENSES OF SUBORDINATES.

SECTION 1. Whenever any Subordinate Lodge shall violate the Constitution, laws, rules or regulations of the Sovereign Grand Lodge, I. O. O. F., or of this Grand Lodge, such Lodge shall be liable to trial and punishment.

SEC. 2. Upon the suspension or expulsion of a Lodge, surrender or forfeiture of its charter, it shall be the duty of its last installed officers and members having the custody of the charter, books, papers, property and funds of the Lodge, to assign, transfer and deliver the same, on demand, to the Grand Master or the District Deputy Grand Master, or to such Past Grand as may be specially deputed by the Grand Master or Grand Lodge to receive them, and the same shall be delivered to the Grand Lodge, and they shall be kept separate and apart from the property of the Grand Lodge, and such funds shall not be estimated as part of the funds of the Grand Lodge, but shall be held in trust for the Subordinate Lodge, to be restored to such Lodge should it be reinstated, or upon the expiration of the period of suspension; *provided*, however, that in the event said Lodge should not be restored to fellowship within three years, the funds of said Lodge shall revert to the General Fund of the Grand Lodge.

SEC. 3. Any Subordinate Lodge failing to hold its meetings for one year, or failing to make its returns, as required by Article XII, Section 1, of this Constitution, shall be deemed an extinct Lodge and its charter shall be forfeited.

SEC. 4. Members of a suspended or expelled Lodge whose charter has been surrendered or forfeited, who were in good standing at the time of such suspension or dissolution, or may have paid all arrearages then due to the

Grand Lodge, shall, upon the recommendation of the District Deputy Grand Master of the District in which the suspended or extinct Lodge is located, receive from the Grand Secretary a certificate, under the seal of the Grand Lodge, to enable them to make application for admission to membership in another Lodge; *provided*, such members are not excluded by Sections 2 and 3 of this Article.

SEC. 5. Upon the application of any five, or more, members of an extinct Lodge, to the Grand Lodge, for the restoration of such Lodge to fellowship, accompanied with satisfactory evidence that a fair opportunity has been given to all who were members in good standing at the time the same became extinct, to unite in such application (except as provided in Section 3 of this Article) such applicants, or such portions thereof as the Grand Lodge may approve of, may be restored to fellowship in said Lodge, together with the charter and effects belonging to such Lodge at the time of its extinction, unless such effects shall have been placed in the General Fund of the Grand Lodge, as provided in Section 2 of this Article.

ARTICLE XIV.

BY-LAWS AND RULES OF ORDER.

SECTION 1. The Grand Lodge may enact such By-laws as may be necessary to carry into effect this Constitution, to regulate the proceedings of its officers and committees, and provide for the safety of its property; and may amend the same by resolution at any annual session, one day's previous notice of the proposed amendment being given.

SEC. 2. The Grand Lodge may make such rules of order as may be necessary for the regulation of its sessions, securing of good order and the dispatch of business. Such rules of order may be suspended at any meeting by a two-thirds' vote; *provided*, that such suspension shall not extend beyond the meeting which voted therefor.

ARTICLE XV.

AMENDMENTS.

This Constitution shall be altered or amended only by a proposition therefor, in writing, submitted at an annual session, which proposition shall set forth the Section proposed to be altered or amended, as it would read when so amended; it shall be entered at length upon the Journal, and shall not be acted upon until the next annual session, when it may be considered and perfected by amendments, and if agreed to by two-thirds of the members present, and voting, shall be adopted.

RULES OF ORDER.

1.—ORDER OF BUSINESS.

The Order of Business for the Annual Session shall be, on the

FIRST DAY.

1st. The Grand Master shall request the members to clothe themselves in proper regalia, and direct the officers to take their respective stations, and fill vacancies *pro tem.*, and shall then, after all have been examined, call up the Grand Lodge.

2d. While standing, the Grand Chaplain shall address the Supreme Ruler of the Universe in prayer.

3d. Proclamation shall be made by the Grand Marshal of the opening of the Grand Lodge.

4th. The Grand Secretary shall present, and read, if required, the credentials of members.

5th. The Committee on Credentials shall forthwith examine and report on the eligibility of members.

6th. New members of the Grand Lodge shall be admitted.

7th. The record of all Special Sessions shall be read and passed upon by the Grand Lodge.

8th. Vacancies in committees and among appointed officers shall be filled.

9th. The reports of the Grand Officers shall be presented and read.

10th. Petitions, Communications, Appeals, and Financial Accounts, shall be presented and referred in the order above mentioned.

11th. Miscellaneous business.

SECOND DAY.

12th. Reading and approval of minutes of preceding day.

13th. Reception and reference of credentials, reports thereon, and admission of new members.

14th. Resolutions of inquiry of Standing or Special Committees.

15th.   Reports of Standing Committees, in the order in which they are named in the Constitution.

16th.   Reports of Special Committees by seniority.

17th.   Consideration of proposed amendments to the Constitution of the Grand Lodge.

18th.   Consideration of proposed amendments to the Constitution of Subordinate Lodges.

19th.   Petitions, Communications, Appeals, and Financial Accounts, presented and referred.

20th.   Unfinished business.

21st.   New business.

THIRD DAY.

22d.   Reading and approving minutes of preceding day.

23d.   Reception and reference of credentials, reports thereon, and admission of new members.

24th.   At 1 o'clock nominations and election of officers.

25th.   Reports of Standing and Special Committees.

26th.   Additional business in the same order as on the second day.

27th.   Should the foregoing order of business not be concluded on the first or second day, it should be commenced on each succeeding day where it left off on the preceding; except that the reading and approval of the minutes, and reception, reference and reports on credentials of members, shall be the first business in order on each day, and that the nomination and election of officers shall immediately follow them on the third day of the session.

28th.   The vote on a motion to close the session shall not be taken until the day succeeding that at which it shall be offered, and shall be in this form: "That when the Grand Lodge adjourns this day, this Annual Session shall stand adjourned *sine die*."

29th.   On the last day of the session, the officers shall be installed and committees appointed, before it shall be declared closed; the minutes of the day shall be read and approved, if correct.

II.—OF DECORUM.

During the continuance of the meeting, the most decorous silence must be observed; the officers and members retaining their respective seats, and no one leaving the room without the permission of the M. W. Grand Master, nor enter without the consent of the R. W. Grand Warden.

No member shall, by conversation or otherwise, interrupt the business of the Grand Lodge, or refuse to obey the Chair. Every Officer and member shall be designated in debate, or otherwise, by his proper office or title, according to his standing in the Order.

No member shall be permitted to vote or speak, unless clothed in regalia appropriate to his rank or station.

III.—OF THE CHAIR.

The Grand Master, while presiding, shall state every question coming before the Grand Lodge, and immediately, before putting it to vote, shall ask, *"Is the Grand Lodge ready for the question?"* Should no member rise to speak, and a majority indicate their readiness, he shall rise to take the question; and after he has risen, no member shall be permitted to speak upon it. He shall pronounce the vote and decisions of the Grand Lodge on all subjects. His decisions on questions of order shall be without debate, unless, entertaining doubts on the point, he invite it. And he shall have the privilege of speaking only on such question from the Chair. When his decision has been appealed from, the question shall be put thus: *"Will the Grand Lodge sustain the Chair in its decision?"*

IV.—OF DEBATE.

Every member, when he speaks or offers a motion, shall rise and respectfully address the Chair. While speaking, he shall confine himself to the question under debate, avoiding all personality and indecorous language, as well as any reflection upon the Grand Lodge or its members.

Should two or more members rise to speak at the same time, the Chair shall decide which shall be entitled to the floor.

No member shall disturb another in his speech, unless to call him to order for words spoken.

If a member, while speaking, shall be called to order, at the request of the Chair he shall cease speaking, and take his seat until the question of order is determined; when, if permitted, he may again proceed.

No member shall speak more than once on the same question, until all the members wishing to speak shall have had an opportunity to do so; nor more than twice without permission of the Chair. But no member shall have the privilege of speaking more than once on a question of order, after appeal from the decision of the Chair.

V.—OF QUESTIONS AND VOTES.

When any communication, petition or memorial is presented, before it is read, or any vote taken on it, a brief statement of its contents shall be made by the introducer or the Chair. And after it has been read, a brief notice of the purport shall be entered on the Journal.

No motion shall be subject to action until seconded and stated by the Chair, and by the desire of any member shall be reduced to writing.

When a blank is to be filled, the question shall be taken first upon the highest sum or number, and the longest or latest time proposed.

Any member may call for a division of a question, when the sense will admit of it.

When a question is before the Grand Lodge, no motion shall be received unless to adjourn, the previous question, to lay on the table, to postpone indefinitely, to postpone to a certain time, to refer, or to amend, and shall have precedence in the order herein arranged; the first three of which shall be decided without debate.

After any question, except one of indefinite postponement, has been decided, any two members who voted in the majority may, during the same communication, move for a reconsideration thereof.

The previous question can be called for by two members, if seconded by five other members, and shall be put in this form : *"Shall the main question be now put ?"* If carried, all debate shall cease, and the vote shall be first upon all pending amendments, beginning with the last one proposed, after which, upon the main question.

When five members rise in favor of taking a question by ayes and noes, they shall be ordered to be so recorded.

Every member present shall vote on any question before the Grand Lodge, unless he is personally interested in the result, or has been excused by the Grand Lodge, or is otherwise incapacitated.

No more than two amendments to a proposition shall be entertained at the same time—that is, an amendment, and an amendment to an amendment—and the question shall be first taken on the latter; *provided*, that when the sense will admit, one substitute to the whole subject matter will be entertained, and the question shall be first taken on the substitute.

When the ayes and noes are ordered, the names of the Representatives shall be called by Lodges.

CONSTITUTION

—OF—

SUBORDINATE LODGES

UNDER THE JURISDICTION OF THE

R. W. GRAND LODGE, I. O. O. F.,

OF THE

STATE OF NEVADA.

———◆———

For the purpose of effecting uniformity in the administration of the privileges, honors and benefits of Odd Fellowship, the Grand Lodge of the Independent Order of Odd Fellows of the State of Nevada ordains the following Constitution for the government of Subordinate Lodges in this jurisdiction :

ARTICLE I.

This Lodge shall consist of at least five members, one of whom shall be in possession of the Third Degree, to be hailed and entitled .... Lodge, No. ...., Independent Order of Odd Fellows of Nevada, holding a legal and unreclaimed charter, granted or sanctioned by the Grand Lodge of the Independent Order of Odd Fellows of the State of Nevada. It cannot voluntarily surrender its charter, or dissolve, so long as five Brothers in good standing object thereto.

ARTICLE II.

MEMBERSHIP.

SECTION 1. All candidates for initiation must be free white males, able to read and write, of the age of twenty-one years and upward, of sound health, of good moral character and industrious habits, having some respectable known means of support, and believe in the existence of a Supreme Being, the Creator and Preserver of the Universe, and be proposed in the Lodge nearest his residence, except that Lodge grant permission for his joining another Lodge; *provided*, that application for membership may be made to any Lodge nearest the residence of the applicant, in the same county or district. A person may be admitted to any Lodge in the city or village in which he resides; but all candidates for initiation must have resided in this State six months, and in the county in which the application is made thirty days prior to the time of making the application, except such candidates as may apply from other States or Territories where there is no Grand Lodge or District Deputy Grand Sire located.

SEC. 2. All candidates for membership by deposit of card, or dismissal certificate, or as Ancient Odd Fellows, whose cards have been granted more than twelve months, shall deposit their cards with the proposition, or furnish satisfactory evidence that such card has been lost.

SEC. 3. No suspended or expelled member of the Order can be admitted to membership in this Lodge, except on a dismissal certificate, or on being reinstated and receiving a withdrawal card from the Lodge which suspended or expelled him; or if a member of a defunct Lodge, a certificate from the Grand Secretary, as prescribed by law, and by the payment of a fee of not less than fifteen dollars, and by signing a petition substantially as follows:

To...... Lodge, No......., I. O. O. F.

The undersigned respectfully represents, that about the year .... he was initiated into ...... Lodge, No. ...., under the jurisdiction of the R. W. Grand Lodge of ......, and city or town of ......; that he has taken .... degrees, and holds the rank of ......

Your petitioner further represents, that he has not been expelled or suspended from any Lodge for misconduct or contempt, and that his connection with the Order was severed by ....

Therefore he prays for admission to your Lodge, and hereby pledges his word of honor that the facts set forth in this petition are true.

Refers to...

Age............., Occupation.... ....

Witness.. { ....
{ ....Petitioner.

SEC. 4. It shall be the duty of the applicant to sign the petition with his full name in the presence of two members of the Lodge he proposes to join, and no petition shall be received into any Lodge without the signature of said witnesses.

SEC. 5. If the report of the investigating committee be favorable, and the candidate be elected, it shall be the duty of the N. G. to appoint an examining committee of three members, one of whom shall, if practicable, be a Past Grand, and the committee shall examine the applicant as to the degrees he has attained and the rank he holds in the Order, and shall report the same to the Lodge; and it shall be the duty of the Secretary to note said report upon the minutes, and upon the adoption of the report by the Lodge the applicant shall be admitted and sign the Constitution and By-Laws.

SEC. 6. If any person shall gain admittance to this Lodge upon a petition containing any false representations, he shall be expelled.

SEC. 7. The name of a person offered for membership, with his age, residence and occupation, must be proposed by a member in writing, signed by the applicant with his full name, with the names of two persons as references attached, and entered upon the record, and forthwith be referred to a committee of three members for investigation, who shall report at the next regular meeting (unless extraordinary circumstances prevent), and signed by a majority of said committee, when the candidate shall be balloted for with ball ballots, and if less than three black balls appear, he shall be elected, but if three or more black balls appear, he shall be rejected.

SEC. 8. No reconsideration of an unfavorable balloting can be had, unless all the Brothers who may cast black balls against an applicant for membership voluntarily make a motion for a reconsideration of the ballot; and in such case the vote on the reconsideration shall be taken by ball ballots, and if all the balls cast be in favor of it, the reconsideration shall be had; whereupon the application shall lie over till the succeeding regular meeting, when another ballot shall be had with ball ballots, and if the same be unanimously in favor of the applicant, he shall thereby be elected; one reconsideration only in the same case shall be allowed, and, provided, always, that such reconsideration shall be had within four meeting nights succeeding the rejection. A favorable balloting can be reconsidered at any meeting prior to the admission of the candidate; *provided*, two-thirds of the members present agree thereto.

SEC. 9. When a candidate has been rejected, notice thereof shall be sent without delay to the R. W. Grand Secretary, and all the Lodges in the District, and he cannot be proposed again in any Lodge for the space of one year after such rejection; *provided*, that upon deposit of a card a Brother can apply at any time.

SEC. 10. A proposition for membership can be withdrawn any time prior to the report of the committee thereon being read to the Lodge. If a person shall be illegally or fraudulently elected a member of this Lodge, at any time previous to the applicant's initiation, the Lodge can, by a majority vote, order a new ballot. In case an illegal ballot is cast, the presiding officer cannot declare the ballot void; it can only be done by a majority vote of the Lodge.

ARTICLE III.

FEES, DUES AND BENEFITS.

SECTION I.   The fees and dues of this Lodge shall not be less than fifteen dollars for initiation; five dollars for admission by card; ten dollars for admission by dismissal certificate, as an ancient Odd Fellow, or as a non-affiliate Odd Fellow; ten dollars each for the first and second degrees; and five dollars for the third degree, and such amount of dues as shall be determined by the by-laws; in addition to which the Lodge may provide for a widows', orphans' and educational fund, and funeral tax, and for extraordinory assessments for Lodge purposes.

SEC. 2.   Every member not over thirteen weeks in arrears to the Lodge for dues, or an aggregate of dues, fines and assessments, to an amount equal to more than thirteen weeks' dues, shall, in case of being disabled by sickness or bodily accident from following his usual occupation, or otherwise earning a livelihood, be entitled to and may receive such weekly benefits from the funds of the Lodge as may be provided by its by-laws; *provided*, such weekly benefits shall not exceed in amount one-half the amount of yearly dues; *and, provided further*, his sickness or disability has not been occasioned by any unnecessary exposure, imprudence or immoral conduct, or not constitutionally diseased prior to his admission to the Lodge; in such cases no benefits can be allowed. Nor will any brother be entitled to benefits until the expiration of six months from the date of his admission. All dues, fines and assessments to be deducted from benefits previous to their payment.

SEC. 3.   Should a Brother's disability be local and apparently permanent, but, his general health not disqualify him from following some occupation by which he can secure a livelihood, he is not entitled to benefits under this Constitution.

SEC. 4.   Any Brother who is in good health, but in arrears for over thirteen weeks, or an aggregate amount including fines and assessments equal to more than thirteen weeks dues, shall not be entitled to any benefits for any sickness or disability that may arise prior to the expiration of four weeks after the payment of said arrearages in full. "Arrears" shall be construed to be the amount in excess of thirteen weeks.

SEC. 5.   In case of the death of a member not over one year in arrears for dues, or an aggregate amount, including fines and assessments, equal to one year's dues, or the wife of such member, there shall be allowed from the Lodge funds not less than thirty dollars to defray the expenses of the burial. In the absence of competent relations, the N. G. shall take charge of the funeral and render an account of the disbursements. Should a deceased brother in good standing, in accordance with Section 2 of this Article, leave a wife and children, or either, they shall be entitled to not less than thirty dollars funeral benefits, to be paid only to said wife and children. All orders for benefits or funeral expenses shall be by vote of the Lodge.

ARTICLE IV.

DEGREES.

SECTION 1. A Brother who has been in membership one month shall be eligible for degrees, but shall not be elected to more than two degrees at the same meeting, unless a dispensation be obtained therefor from the Grand Master, or his Deputy for the District.

SEC. 2. Application for election to any of the degrees of a Subordinate Lodge shall be accompanied with the amount required therefor, and shall be presented to the Lodge when open in that order of business, if so provided; if not, in the order of new business; and when the Lodge has regularly closed, it shall then forthwith open in the degrees and ballot upon the application, and if the ballot be fair, the applicant shall be entitled to receive said degrees at any time appointed by the Noble Grand; but if one black ball shall appear, the application shall lie over until the next succeeding meeting of the Lodge in the same degree, when a new ballot shall be taken, and if three or more black balls appear, the degree applied for shall be refused, and the applicant shall be debarred from renewing his application for six months; but if less than three black balls appear, the applicant shall be elected to receive said degrees.

SEC. 3. This Lodge may also confer the Degree of Rebekah on all Third Degree members in good standing, their wives, widows of members in good standing at the time of their death, the unmarried legally adopted daughters, sisters, and the widowed sisters of Third Degree members; *provided*, that the daughters and sisters of members shall have attained the age of eighteen years, and are recommended by their parents, guardian, or their brother.

ARTICLE V.

OFFICERS.

SECTION 1. The elective officers of this Lodge shall consist of a Noble Grand, Vice Grand, Secretary and Treasurer, who shall serve a regular term each, and the Lodge may elect a Permanent Secretary for the same time, or for one year, to take charge of the accounts between the Lodge and its members.
4

SEC. 2. The appointed officers shall consist of a Warden, Conductor, Outside Guardian, Inside Guardian, Right Supporter of Noble Grand, Left Supporter of Noble Grand, Right Supporter of Vice Grand, Left Supporter of Vice Grand, and Right and Left S. Supporters, who shall each serve a regular term; and the N. G. may also appoint a Chaplain for a regular term.

SEC. 3. No member shall be installed as N. G., unless he has served a term as V. G., or the last of a term to fill a vacancy; nor as V. G., unless he has served a term or a majority of the nights of a term, including the last night, in an inferior office, other than Permanent Secretary or Chaplain; such service in office, whether elected or appointed in any other Lodge, is qualifying; *provided*, a Brother has a certificate to that effect, under seal of a Lodge in good standing; *provided*, that any Third Degree member may be elected if all qualified Brothers refuse to serve, and a dispensation be granted by the M. W. Grand Master, Deputy Grand Master, or Deputy of the District, previous to the election.

SEC. 4. The N. G. and V. G. must each be in possession of the Degree of Rebekah, and all elective and appointed officers shall be clear of all pecuniary charges on the books, and have attained the Third Degree previous to installation.

SEC. 5. Nominations for Elective Officers shall be made only on the two regular meetings immediately preceding that of the regular election, except when the nominees for an office all decline. There having been but one candidate, and he having been beaten by blank ballots, the N. G. shall declare the candidate out of nomination.

SEC. 6. Officers shall be elected at the last regular meeting in each term, and be installed at the first regular meeting in the new term; *provided*, the installing officer be present; if absent, the Lodge may, by vote, defer it for one week, or call a special meeting for the purpose at the request of the D. D. Grand Master.

SEC. 7. Any officer absenting himself from the Lodge for three successive meetings, except in case of sickness, or any officer for misconduct or neglect, as such, may be removed by a vote of two-thirds of the members voting at the next regular meeting after a resolution therefor has been offered in the Lodge.

SEC. 8. Vacancies in any elective office may be filled by the Lodge by nomination and election at the next regular meeting after nominating; and until so filled, the N. G. shall appoint a member to the office, pro tem.

SEC. 9. The duties of the various officers shall be as laid down in the charges of office, and as specified by this Constitution and the by-laws of the Lodge.

SEC. 10. The N. G., or officer acting as such, shall appoint the majority, and the V. G., or the officer acting as such, the minority of all committees on candidates and charges.

SEC. 11. The Lodge shall, at its first regular meeting in April of each year, elect three Representatives to the Grand Lodge for its charter, and one for each fifteen members, as shown by its report on the 31st day of December of the previous year.

SEC. 12. Representatives must be Past Grands in good standing in the Lodge at the time of their election, and shall hold their office for one year from the date of the meeting of the Grand Lodge. Should a vacancy occur it may be filled by an election at any regular meeting of the Lodge previous to the annual session of the R. W. Grand Lodge.

ARTICLE VI.

SECTION 1. A member to be entitled to the term pass-word at the beginning of a term must have paid all dues, fines and assessments against him to that date; and a member who is in arrears for dues more than thirteen weeks, or an aggregate of dues, fines and assessments to an amount equal to more than thirteen weeks' dues, shall not be entitled to weekly or funeral benefits, nor to vote or speak in the Lodge, but may visit his own Lodge until dropped from membership, suspended or expelled in accordance with law. The Lodge cannot refuse to receive any part of the dues of a member prior to the time he is dropped from membership, and no member can be dropped from membership for non-payment of dues, unless at the time of being dropped he shall be indebted to the Lodge for more than one year's dues. Any member eleven months in arrears for dues shall be notified by the Secretary of the Lodge of the condition of his account. If he still neglect payment, at the end of one year the Secretary shall so report to the N. G. of the Lodge, when the N. G. shall read the Brother's name for the first time as liable to be dropped from membership, The matter shall then lie over for one week, when, if no payment has been made, the N. G. shall declare him dropped from membership, unless the Lodge shall otherwise decide. The fact of a member being over twelve months in arrears does not constitute him a dropped member. To render him such, the Lodge must formally declare him to be dropped.

SEC. 2. Any member who shall violate any of the principles of the Order, the Constitution, By-laws or Rules of Order of this Lodge, or who shall knowingly propose an unworthy applicant for membership, be guilty of immorality, feign sickness with a view to abuse the benevolent intentions of the Order, or shall divulge, except to a member of the Order legally entitled to the same, any of the proceedings of this Lodge or of the Order required to be kept secret, shall be reprimanded, suspended (not to exceed two years), or expelled, as the Lodge may determine.

SEC. 3. Any member of a Subordinate Lodge within this jurisdiction, who shall, upon due trial, be convicted of using intoxicating liquors to such an extent as to cause him to habitually neglect his family or business, shall be considered a common drunkard, and shall be expelled from the Order.

SEC. 4. Notice of all suspensions, expulsions, rejections, reinstatements, and of Brothers dropped from membership, shall forthwith be forwarded to every Lodge in the District, and to the Subordinate Encampment, of which the Lodge shall have been notified of such Brother having become a member; also, to the R. W. Grand Secretary.

SEC. 5. Every member shall be entitled to a fair trial for any offense involving reprimand, suspension or expulsion. No member shall be put upon trial unless charges, prepared in strict accordance with the code of procedure regulating charges and trials, shall be submitted to the Lodge, in writing, and signed by a member of the Order in good standing.

ARTICLE VII.

SECTION 1. Any person who may have ceased to be a member in consequence of non-payment of dues, may be reinstated within one year, by a vote of two-thirds of the members present—the motion to that effect having been laid over one week—by the payment of the amount due the Lodge at the time he ceased to be a member; but *after* one year, the amount due the Lodge shall be paid, and he shall petition the Lodge, in writing to be reinstated, which shall be disposed of, in *all respects*, as provided for in Article II, Section 7, for petitions for membership by initiation.

SEC. 2. Applications for reinstatement, by card, by dismissal certificate, as an Ancient or non-affiliated Odd Fellow, shall be made by petition at a regular meeting, and shall be accompanied by the required fee.

SEC. 3. Non-affiliated Odd Fellows who have been regularly initiated in the Order, and have retained membership therein for five consecutive years, and who, at the time of making application for reinstatement shall be over fifty years of age, may be admitted to membership as non-beneficial members; such members to be subject to the payment of one dollar for admission and such dues as the by-laws of the Lodge may prescribe.

SEC. 4. A member of the Order having been for twenty-five years a contributing member, may be admitted to membership in this Lodge without first applying for a withdrawal card from the Lodge in which he holds membership; *provided*, that, upon election to membership in this Lodge, the Secretary shall notify the Lodge of which the Brother is a member of such election, whereupon, a withdrawal card having been granted to the Brother and the same deposited in this Lodge, he shall be entitled to all the privileges of membership upon sign-ing the Constitution and By-Laws and the payment of the required admission fee.

ARTICLE VIII.

FUNDS AND PROPERTY.

This Lodge has jurisdiction over its financial affairs so long as it acts in obedience to its charter or dispensation, and of this Constitution and the laws of the Order. The funds and property of this Lodge are " trust funds," to be devoted to no other purpose than the charitable uses of the I. O. O. F., and expenditures legitimately made for Lodge purposes, and the advancement of the interests of the Lodge or the Order. The funds may be invested, from time to time, as the Lodge shall direct, but no part thereof, or of the Lodge property, or of the proceeds of any sales of such property, shall ever be divided among the members, either directly or under the disguise of a loan to a member, or members; and in case of a surrender or forfeiture of the Lodge charter, all the funds and property of the Lodge, of whatsoever kind, shall be immediately surrendered and delivered up to the R. W. Grand Lodge of this jurisdiction, or to its officers or agents properly authorized to receive them.

ARTICLE IX.

OFFENSES.

SECTION 1. No member of this Lodge shall be concerned in organizing or visiting any illegal, spurious, expelled, extinct or suspended Lodge of Odd Fellows; nor paint on his sign any emblem of the Order, or otherwise exhibit any upon the same, or have any printed or engraved upon his business card, or expose in any public place as a sign; nor receive or put any motion from the chair of the N. G. unless he be a Present or Past N. G., or V. G., or R. S. of the N. G., occupying the chair during the temporary absence of the N. G.

SEC. 2. This Lodge shall not have a public procession unless to attend the funeral of a member or have any public celebration of any kind, or get up any ball or public amusement in the name of the Order, without permission of the Grand Master, or admit to membership any member of an expelled or extinct Lodge, or reinstate an expelled or suspended member of this Lodge without permission of the Grand Lodge.

ARTICLE X.

TERMS AND RETURNS.

SECTION 1. All terms shall commence on the 1st day of January and the 1st day of July of each year, and end June 30th and December 31st; *provided,* that this shall not be construed so as to affect Lodges who have the permit of the R. W. Grand Lodge to meet twice a month; their terms to be one year, and shall commence January 1st and end December 31st of each year.

SEC. 2. The officers for the term about expiring shall prepare and deliver to the officer who shall install their successors the result of the elections and a regular report of the work of the term, including the names of the initiated, admitted by card, and as an Ancient Odd Fellow; those suspended or expelled, and the cause thereof, and those reinstated and deceased; the number of certificates for Degrees granted; the whole number in membership, and the amount of receipts, accompanied by whatever amount may be due to the Grand Lodge. They shall annually make to the Grand Lodge a full return of members of the Lodge, ranked according to the Degrees attained, and a statement of the number of members relieved in the past year; the number of widowed families relieved; the number of members buried; the number of sisters buried; the amount of money applied to each of these purposes, designating the amount paid for the education of orphans; the amount of money in the treasury; amount of widows' and orphans' fund, and the amount of investments.

SEC. 3. Should the Lodge fail to make any of these returns for one year, it shall thereby forfeit its charter and become extinct, and it shall be the duty of the G. Master or D. D. G. M. to withhold the A. T. P. W. and the term P. W. until such returns are made and the amount due the Grand Lodge is paid. And it shall be the duty of the last installed officers to transmit or surrender to the Grand Master or his Deputy the charter, books, papers, furniture, funds and other property of the Lodge.

ARTICLE XI.

CARDS AND CERTIFICATES.

SECTION 1. Applications for cards must be made in open Lodge, either in person or in writing. All dues, fines or assessments must be paid in full up to the time for which a visiting card is granted, and a withdrawal card cannot be granted to a member who is not clear of the books.

SEC. 2. A withdrawal card, as soon as granted, relieves the Lodge from all liability for benefits, whether the card be taken or not.

SEC. 3. A visiting card cannot be granted for more than one year.

SEC. 4. On application therefor, the Lodge may, by a two-thirds' vote, grant a card to the wife of a member in good standing, or the widow of a member in good standing at the time of his death; such card cannot be granted to a wife for more than one year, but when granted to a widow shall be valid during her widowhood.

Sec. 5. When a Brother who has been dropped for non-payment of dues applies for reinstatement, and the application is rejected, he shall be entitled to, and the Lodge shall grant him, a dismissal certificate upon the payment of one dollar.

Sec. 6. A withdrawal card must be granted by ball ballots. A ballot by which a withdrawal card is granted cannot be reconsidered or rescinded.

ARTICLE XII.

APPEALS.

An appeal from the action of the Lodge on a decision of law only may be taken at any time within two weeks after the decision, upon filing with the Secretary notice of appeal, and the grounds thereof, whereupon the Secretary shall forthwith send a certified copy of the same to the D. D. G. M.

ARTICLE XIII.

BY-LAWS.

Section 1. This Lodge may make, alter or rescind such By-laws, Rules or Resolutions, from time to time, as may be deemed expedient; *provided*, that they do not contravene this Constitution, or the Constitution, By-laws or Regulations of the Grand Lodge of the State of Nevada or of the Sovereign Grand Lodge; *and, provided further*, that when an amendment is proposed, the Section proposed to be amended shall be set forth at length as it would read should the proposed amendment be adopted.

Sec. 2. The By-laws of this Lodge shall not go into force and effect until duly approved by the Committee on Laws of Subordinates, and the manuscript copy of such By-laws shall, before being printed, be transmitted to the Grand Secretary, to be submitted to the said committee for their approval.

ARTICLE XIV.

AMENDMENTS AND INTERPRETATIONS.

Section 1. When any doubt arises of the true meaning of any part of these Articles, it shall be determined by the Grand Lodge.

Sec. 2. These Articles, or any part thereof, shall not be altered, amended, suspended or annulled except by a majority vote of the R. W. Grand Lodge at a regular session.

CONSTITUTION

DEGREE OF REBEKAH LODGES

SUBORDINATE TO THE

R. W. GRAND LODGE, I. O. O. F.,

OF THE

STATE OF NEVADA,

As Adopted at the Fifteenth Annual Session, 1881.

———————

For the purpose of effecting uniformity in the administration of the privileges, benefits and honors of the Rebekah Degree, I. O. O. F., within this jurisdiction, the Right Worthy Grand Lodge of the Independent Order of Odd Fellows of the State of Nevada ordains the following Constitution for Rebekah Degree Lodges under its jurisdiction :

ARTICLE I.

This Lodge shall consist of seven members in good standing, including one qualified to preside at its meetings, to be hailed and entitled .... Degree of Rebekah Lodge, No. ...., Independent Order of Odd Fellows of the State of Nevada, holding a legal and unreclaimed charter granted or sanctioned by the Grand Lodge of the Independent Order of Odd Fellows of the

5

State of Nevada. It cannot voluntarily surrender its charter so long as seven (7) members object thereto.

ARTICLE II.

This Lodge shall have power to confer the Degree of Rebekah on all Scarlet Degree members of the Order who present a certificate of good standing from their Lodges; the wives of Scarlet Degree members in good standing; the widows of Odd Fellows presenting a certificate from a Lodge of which their husbands were members in good standing at the time of their death; the unmarried daughters, unmarried sisters and widowed sisters of Scarlet Degree members, who have attained the age of eighteen years, upon the recommendation of their parents, guardian, or their brother.

ARTICLE III.

OF MEETINGS.

This Lodge shall hold regular meetings twice each month, and special meetings as prescribed by the By-laws.

ARTICLE IV.

PROPOSITIONS FOR MEMBERSHIP.

SECTION 1. The name of a person offered for membership, with his or her name, residence and occupation, must be proposed by a member, in writing, signed by the applicant, with the names of two persons as references attached and entered upon the record, and forthwith be referred to a committee of three members for investigation, who shall report at the next succeeding regular meeting (unless extraordinary circumstances prevent), when the candidate shall be balloted for with ball ballots, and, if three or more black balls appear, the applicant shall be declared rejected, but, if less than three black balls appear, the applicant shall be declared elected; *provided*, that no applicant shall be admitted to membership in this Lodge, or to sign the Constitution and By-laws, until the next succeeding regular meeting thereafter. Applicants by card or dismissal certificates shall be disposed of in the same manner.

SEC. 2. No reconsideration of an unfavorable balloting can be had, unless all the members who cast the black balls against an applicant for membership voluntarily make a motion for a reconsideration of the ballot, and in such a case the vote on the reconsideration shall be taken by ball ballots, and, if all the balls cast be in favor of it, the reconsideration shall be had; whereupon the application shall lie over until the next succeeding regular meeting, when another ballot shall be had with ball ballots, and, if the same be unanimously in favor of the applicant, he or she shall be elected, but, if one or more black balls appear in either ballot, the applicant shall be rejected, and never more than one motion for a reconsideration shall be allowed. A favorable balloting can be reconsidered at any meeting prior to the admission of the candidate; *provided*, a majority of the members present agree thereto.

SEC. 3. To be in good standing in this Lodge it is necessary that a Brother shall be in good standing in his Subordinate Lodge. A Sister to be in good standing must be free from all charges on the books of this Lodge, financially or otherwise.

SEC. 4. A member to be entitled to the S. A. P. W., at the beginning of a term, must have paid all dues against him or her to that date; and a member of this Lodge who is in arrears for weekly or funeral dues more than thirteen weeks is not entitled to speak or vote in the Lodge, but is a contributing member until dropped from membership, or expelled; and as such is entitled to visit his or her own Lodge. He or she cannot, however, become entitled to benefits until he or she shall have paid up in full all dues and fines—weekly and funeral— that have accrued against him or her up to the date of payment, nor then, until the expiration of such time thereafter as may by the laws be provided as a penalty.

SEC. 5. This Lodge cannot refuse to receive, in full or in part, the dues of a member prior to the time he or she ceased to be a member, and no member can be suspended or dropped from membership for non-payment of dues, unless at the time he or she is dropped they shall be indebted to the Lodge for more than one year's dues. Any member of this Lodge who shall neglect or refuse to pay the dues fixed by law, for the space of one year, shall be reported by the Secretary to the Noble Grand, and, unless the Lodge shall otherwise direct, such member shall thereupon be dropped from membership, he or she having first been notified of the action that would be taken, a record of which shall be made upon the minutes. The mere fact of a member being over twelve months in arrears does not constitute him or her a dropped member. To render them such, the Lodge must formally declare them to have ceased membership.

SEC. 6. Any member who has ceased membership for non-payment of dues may be reinstated within one year by a two-thirds' vote of the members present at any regular meeting, by payment of the amount due the Lodge at the time of suspension, a motion to that effect having laid over one meeting. After the lapse of one year, application must be made in accordance with Section I of this Article, and upon payment of one year's dues.

SEC. 7. When a candidate has been rejected, notice thereof shall be sent without delay to the Grand Secretary and to all the Degree of Rebekah Lodges in this jurisdiction.

ARTICLE V.

OFFICERS.

SECTION 1. The elective officers of this Lodge shall consist of a Noble Grand, Vice Grand, Secretary and Treasurer, who shall serve a regular term each, and the Lodge may elect a Permanent Secretary for the same time, or for one year, to take charge of the accounts between the Lodge and its members.

SEC. 2. The appointed officers shall consist of a Warden, Conductor, Outside Guardian, Inside Guardian, Right Supporter of Noble Grand, Left Supporter of Noble Grand, Right Supporter of Vice Grand and Left Supporter of Vice Grand, who shall serve a regular term; and the Lodge may also appoint a Chaplain for a regular term.

SEC. 3. No member shall be installed N. G., unless he or she shall: First, be an actual contributing member in good standing in the Lodge; second, no member shall be eligible to the office of N. G., unless previous service is shown in the office of V. G. in a Degree of Rebekah or Subordinate Lodge. The other elective and appointed officers shall be members of this Lodge in good standing.

SEC. 4. Officers of the Lodge shall be clear of all pecuniary charges on the books of whatever kind previous to installation.

SEC. 5. Nominations for elective officers shall be made at the meeting immediately preceding that of the regular election, and also on the night of the election. There having been but one candidate, and he or she having been beaten by blank ballots, the Noble Grand shall declare the candidate out of nomination.

SEC. 6. Officers shall be elected at the last regular meeting in each term, and be installed at the first regular meeting in the new term; *provided*, the installing officer be present; if absent, the Lodge may, by vote, defer it for one week, or call a special meeting for the purpose, at the request of the D. D. Grand Master.

SEC. 7. Any officer being absent from the Lodge for three successive meetings, except in case of sickness, or any officer for misconduct or neglect, may be removed by a vote of two-thirds of the members present at the next meeting, after a resolution has been offered for that purpose in the Lodge.

SEC. 8. Vacancies in any elective office may be filled by the Lodge by nomination, and election at the next regular meeting after nominating, and until so filled the N. G. shall appoint a member to the office, *pro tem.*

SEC. 9. The duties of the various officers shall be as laid down in the charges of office, and as specified by this Constitution and the By-laws of the Lodge.

SEC. 10. The N. G., or officer acting as such, shall appoint the majority, and the V. G., or officer acting as such, the minority of all committees on candidates and charges.

SEC. 11. No member of this Lodge shall be concerned in organizing or visiting any illegal, spurious, expelled, extinct, or suspended Lodges of Odd Fellows; nor paint on his or her sign any emblem of the Order, or otherwise exhibit any upon the same, or have any printed or engraved upon his or her business card, nor expose in a public place as a sign.

ARTICLE VI.

TERMS AND RETURNS.

SECTION 1. All terms shall commence on January 1st and July 1st of each year, and end on June 30th and December 31st of each year.

SEC. 2. The officers for the term about expiring shall prepare and deliver to the officer who shall install their successors the result of the elections, and a regular report of the work for the term, including the number of members, and shall make an annual report in full to the Grand Lodge of all dues and receipts, also of all benefits and expenses for the year.

ARTICLE VII.

REVENUE.

This Lodge may provide for a revenue in its By-laws, by fixing quarterly dues, and fines and penalties upon its officers and members; *provided*, that the admission fee be not less than two dollars.

ARTICLE VIII.

BENEFITS.

The Lodge may, by its By-laws, provide for the payment of such weekly and funeral benefits as they may deem proper.

ARTICLE IX.

FUNDS.

There shall be but one fund in this Lodge, to be called the General Fund, which shall consist of the moneys, stocks and other securities belonging to the Lodge, to be held exclusively as a trust fund, to be devoted to no other purpose than the charitable uses of the I. O. O. F. The funds may be invested, from time to time, as the Lodge may direct, but no part thereof, or of the Lodge property, or of the proceeds of any sales of such property, shall ever be divided among the members; and in case of a surrender or forfeiture of the

Lodge charter, all the funds and property of the Lodge, of whatsoever kind, shall be immediately surrendered and delivered up to the R. W. Grand Lodge of this jurisdiction, or to its officers or agents legally authorized to receive them.

ARTICLE X.

CARDS.

SECTION 1. A withdrawal card cannot be granted to any member who is not clear of the books.

SEC. 2. Visiting cards shall be applied for in open Lodge, and the dues must be paid up to the time for which the card is to be granted.

SEC. 3. A Brother or a Sister who has received the Degree of Rebekah may be admitted to membership in this Lodge, upon the presentation of proper withdrawal cards or dismissal certificates from a Rebekah Degree Lodge, or a certificate from a Subordinate Lodge.

ARTICLE XI.

DISMISSAL CERTIFICATES.

Any member having been dropped from membership for non-payment of dues shall be entitled to receive a dismissal certificate, and the N. G. and Secretary shall issue the same upon the payment of one dollar.

ARTICLE XII.

Charges and trials shall be made and conducted in strict conformity with the Code adopted by the Grand Lodge of the State of Nevada and the provisions of this Constitution.

ARTICLE XIII.

BY-LAWS.

SECTION 1. This Lodge may make, alter or rescind such By-laws, rules and resolutions, from time to time, as may be deemed expedient; *provided*, that they do in no wise contravene this Constitution, or the Constitution, By-laws or regulations of the Grand Lodge of the State of Nevada, or of the Sovereign Grand Lodge.

SEC. 2. The By-laws of this Lodge, or amendments thereto, shall not go into force and effect until duly approved by the Committee on Laws of Subordinates, and the manuscript copy of such By-laws shall, before being printed, be transmitted to the Grand Secretary, to be submitted to said committee for their approval.

CODE OF PROCEDURE

REGULATING

Charges,Trials and Appeals from Proceedings thereunder.

CHARGES AND SPECIFICATIONS.

The charges must clearly set forth the offense committed, and must be in form as follows :

CHARGES.

To.............. ......*Lodge, No*...., *I. O. O. F.*:

The undersigned, a member of............ .....Lodge, No..., I. O. O. F., under the jurisdiction of the R. W. Grand Lodge, I. O. O. F., of the State of Nevada, hereby charges Bro. ...., a member of............. Lodge, No.. , with having been guilty of............, as more fully appears by the following specifications :

Specification First.

Specification Second.

Specification Third.

The specifications must be brief, clear and explicit, and state the offense of which the Brother is accused with precision and certainty.

The facts which are distinct in their nature must be presented in separate and distinct specifications.

Every fact specified must be alleged to have been done on or about a particular day and at a particular place.

The charges and specifications must be entered in full on the minutes of the Lodge.

TRIAL COMMITTEE.

The Trial Committee shall be appointed as provided by Sec. 10, Art. VI, Constitution of Subordinates, and shall consist of five members, who must be, if possible, the peers of the accused. (Sec. 4, Art. VII, Const. of Sub.)

The committee shall organize as soon as possible by electing a Chairman and Secretary, and shall cause to be served upon the accused a notice and summons, in form as follows :

SUMMONS.

....LODGE, No...., I. O. O. F.,}
..........., ..., 18.. }

To......................... ....

SIR AND BROTHER : You are hereby notified that on the........... ...day of.............. A. D. 18.., charges and specifications—of which a certified copy under seal of the Lodge is herewith served on you—were preferred against you and filed in said Lodge, and were referred for trial to the under-signed committee.

You are hereby summoned to appear before said committee at.......... on the ...... day of.............., A. D. 18.., at ,.... o'clock .. M. of that day, to make answer to said charges and proceed with the trial thereof. In default of which you will be reported to said Lodge as being guilty of contempt thereof.

.... •
.... }
.... } *Committee.*
.... }
.... }

SUMMONS—[ENDORSEMENT.]

To......................... ...

....

Filed this .... day of....... ...., A. D. 18..

....
Secretary of Committee.

....LODGE, No...., I. O. O. F.,}
................., 18.. }

I hereby certify that on the........day of.............. A. D. 18.., at the................., State of Nevada, I served the within summons, also

the charges and specifications referred to therein, by delivering to and leaving
with said......:........., the accused, a copy of said summons, attached
to a copy of the charges and specifications against him, under the seal of the
Lodge.

....

Member of said Lodge.

Or, if the accused will admit service, endorse the following :

...., 18..

I hereby admit due service of the within summons, also of a duly certified
copy, under the seal of the Lodge, of the charges and specifications referred to
herein, this......day of................, A. D. 18..

....

Witnesses for the prosecution and defense shall be summoned to appear
before the committee, in form as follows :

. SUBPŒNA.

.................Lodge, No.....I. O. O. F.,}
.....................18...

To....................................

You are hereby notified and required to appear before the committee heretofore appointed to try the charges preferred by Bro........................
against Bro..................at..................on the........day
of..............A. D. 18..., at...o'clock...M., of that day, to testify as
a witness therein on behalf of said...............................

By order of the committee,

....

Secretary of the Committee.

. SUBPŒNA—[ENDORSEMENT.]

To...............................

.................Lodge, No...., I. O. O. F.,}
.................18...

I hereby certify that on the ......day of..............A. D. 18..., I
served the within Subpœna on ....by delivering to and leaving with
him a copy thereof in the...........county of...........

....

Member of said Lodge.

Or,

I hereby accept service of the within Subpœna at.......................
this.......day of..............A. D. 18. .

....

REPORT OF COMMITTEE.

As soon as practicable after the trial has closed the committee shall report to the Lodge in form as follows :

REPORT.

To ....*Lodge, No* ..., *I. O. O. F.:*

Your committee heretofore appointed to try the charges preferred against Bro ....by Bro ...., report that the accompanying documents contain the proceedings of, and the evidence taken before said committee.

That from all that appeared to said committee in said case they find Bro ....

$$\left.\begin{array}{l} .... \\ ....,.... .... \\ .... \\ .... \\ .... \end{array}\right\}\ \textit{Committee.}$$

The report of the committee shall be spread upon the minutes of the Lodge and the Secretary shall forthwith notify the Brother of the same, which notice shall be in form as follows :

NOTICE OF FILING REPORT.

....LODGE, No ..., I. O. O. F.,}
.... 18...

To ....

SIR AND BROTHER : Take notice that the committee heretofore appointed to try charges preferred against you by Bro .... .have this day filed their report and find .... You have two weeks from the date of receiving this notice within which to file your exceptions thereto.

Yours, in F., L. and T.,

....,..... ....
Recording Secretary.

NOTICE OF FILING REPORT—[ENDORSEMENT.]

To ....

....LODGE, No ..., I. O. O. F.,}
. . .. 18...

I hereby certify that I served the within notice on. .... .by

delivering to and leaving with him a copy thereof, this ...... day of ....
A. D. 18.. , at the place aforesaid.

....

Recording Secretary.

If the Brother files exceptions, they shall be in form as follows :

BILL OF EXCEPTIONS.

.... 18...

To .... *Lodge, No*..., *I. O. O. F.:*

The undersigned hereby presents the following Bill of Exceptions to the report of the committee heretofore made herein in relation to the charges preferred against him by Bro............ ; also to the proceedings of and the testimony taken before said committee; also to the action and proceedings of said Lodge in relation to said charges.

First—Said charges and specifications are insufficient to show the commission of the offense charged against the accused herein in this ....
....

Second—The evidence is insufficient to sustain said charges or the report of the committee herein in this.. ....
....

Third—The following errors were committed by the committee in the course of the trial : ....
....

If no exceptions are filed within the time specified, the Lodge shall proceed as provided in Sec. 6, Article VII, of the Constitution of Subordinates.

APPEALS.

An appeal to the Grand Lodge from the judgment of the Lodge may be taken at any time within two weeks after the rendering of said judgment, upon filing with the Secretary of the Lodge notice of appeal, and the grounds thereof, which shall be in form as follows :

NOTICE OF APPEAL.

To .... *Lodge, No*...., *I. O. O. F.:*

Take notice that the undersigned hereby appeals from the action and judgment of this Lodge in the matter of charges preferred against him by Bro. ...., on the following grounds: ....

....

Yours, in F., L. and T.,

....

Dated .... , 18..

If no notice of appeal be given within the time specified, then the judgment of the Lodge shall be final. (Sec. 4, Art. VII, Const. of Sub.)

No appeal can be taken except from a final decision. (Sec. 95, Digest S. G. L.)

In all cases of appeal the Secretary shall transmit, under seal of the Lodge, to the Grand Secretary, certified copies of the following papers : 1st, the charges and specifications; 2d, the testimony and the report of the committee; 3d, the exceptions filed to the report of the committee; 4th, the action of the Lodge on the exceptions and the report of the committee; 5th, the notice of appeal and grounds thereof.

TRIAL.

All exceptions to the formation of a Trial Committee, or challenges for bias or previously-formed opinion, must be made before the Lodge prior to the commencement of the trial. If the exceptions are sustained by the Lodge, another Brother shall be substituted.

Any Brother on trial must have allowed him a fair opportunity for defense and be permitted to present any matter in mitigation.

A Brother on trial must have an opportunity, personally or by counsel, to cross-examine witnesses. (Sec. 1,832, Digest S. G. L.)

If a member refuse to stand trial, he cannot be formally tried, and in such case a Lodge may expel for contempt. (Sec. 1,842, Digest S. G. L.)

If a Brother confesses his guilt, it is not necessary to proceed to trial, but the Trial Committee shall state the fact in their report, and the Lodge shall proceed as in other cases.

When charges have been preferred against a Brother remote from his Lodge, and he answers the summons, denying the charge and stating his inability to attend the trial and to procure counsel, the Lodge shall appoint some competent and disinterested Brother as counsel for the absent Brother, and shall proceed to try the case in the form prescribed.

The general principles and usages of the Order forbid that a person not a member of the Order in good standing should act as counsel before a committee while trying a Brother under charges.

In case of the absence or concealment of a Brother against whom charges have been preferred, so that a copy of the same, or notice of trial, cannot be personally served upon him, a copy of each should be sent to the Postoffice nearest his last known residence, and a copy left at such residence, if the same be known, and upon proof of that fact the Lodge may proceed with the trial, a competent and disinterested Brother having been appointed as counsel for the accused; *provided*, that such papers shall be deemed to have been served upon the Brother only from the date when the constructive service above prescribed is complete; *and provided further*, that in case such Brother returns after the conclusion of his trial, not having appeared on such trial either in person or by counsel of his own choosing, and asks for a new trial, the same shall be granted him, and the testimony of any witness given at the former trial may be used at the second trial, provided the attendance of such witness cannot be had.

OF EVIDENCE.

While an *ex-parte* statement may be regarded as evidence sufficient to place a Brother on his trial, it cannot for one moment be supposed that such testimony is to be permitted on the trial, as such a course would tend to prevent a full and fair investigation of the charges, and thereby defeat not only one of the established rules of law, but be a manifest injustice to the character of the accused, and in violation of his constitutional rights. (Sec. 632, Digest S. G. L.)

The testimony of a wife, for or against her husband, cannot be allowed. (Sec. 632, Digest S. G. L.)

No hearsay evidence should be permitted.

If for any reason the prosecution has failed to produce material evidence before the evidence for the defense has commenced, it is still competent to allow new evidence to be introduced by the prosecution at any time before the case is finally submitted for decision. Justice requires that each party be allowed to introduce all competent evidence, without regard to the time when such evidence is offered.

No testimony against a Brother, taken by any committee without notice to him, and in his absence, should be received, except as hereinbefore provided.

Whenever a Subordinate Lodge, or a member under charges, shall desire to take the testimony of a witness whose personal presence cannot be had before the committee trying said charges, his deposition may be taken in the following manner : The party desiring to take the deposition shall file with the Secretary of the Lodge the interrogatories he wishes to be propounded to the witness or witnesses, naming them, which shall be in form as follows :

In the matter of Charges by Bro..against
Bro...

To the Secretary of.................Lodge, No..., I. O. O. F.:

Please take notice that the undersigned requires that a commission issue out of said Lodge, directed to...to take the testimony of.... ...., a witness on behalf of ...., residing at................. ...., and files herewith the following interrogatories, to be propounded to said witness :

Interrogatory first ....

Interrogatory second.. ..

(Signed)   ....

The Secretary shall deliver or cause to be delivered to the opposite party a copy of the notice and interrogatories. The latter party, within one week from such service, may file counter interrogatories with the Secretary, if he or they think proper, which shall be in form as follows :

In the matter of Bro ....*against*
Bro... ....

Counter interrogatories to be propounded to Bro...................... .... :
a witness on behalf of........................ ....

Counter interrogatory first..

Counter interrogatory second...... ....

(Signed)   ....

At the expiration of the week, or sooner, if counter interrogatories be sooner filed, the Secretary shall forthwith forward them to the Noble Grand of a Lodge near the witness, with a commission authorizing and requesting him to take the deposition of the witness or witnesses named, which commission shall be in form as follows :

COMMISSION TO TAKE TESTIMONY.

HALL OF.................LODGE, No. ..., I. O. O. F.

To the N. G. of.................*Lodge, No. .., I. O. O. F.:*

You are hereby authorized and requested to take the testimony of........
.............., a witness in the matter of charges by Bro................
against Bro......................., by first requiring him to relate the truth and whole truth, upon the honor of an Odd Fellow ; then propounding the interrogatories hereto annexed, separate and in succession, taking his answers in writing as given ; then by requiring him to attest the same by his signature, and date, and finally by affixing your certificate, under the seal of your Lodge, that the testimony was duly taken according to law.

....
Recording Secretary.

[SEAL OF LODGE.]

The Secretary shall attach the papers in the following order :

1st.   Commission.

2d.   Interrogatories.

3d.   Counter interrogatories.

Upon the receipt of the same the Noble Grand shall, as soon as possible, take or cause the deposition to be taken by some competent member of the Order, causing every interrogatory to be propounded to the witness, and the answers to each reduced to writing in the presence of the witness, and when the deposition is completed, shall cause the witness to sign the same, and then the Noble Grand, or the person taking the same, shall certify the same to be duly taken, which certificates shall be in form as follows :

....Lodge, No. .., I. O. O. F., }
...., 18

I hereby certify that Bro ...., the person named as a witness in the foregoing papers, personally appeared before me this day, and after first being by me obligated upon the honor of an Odd Fellow, testified and made answer as heretofore set forth, and as signed by him in my presence.

Dated this......day of.... ...., A. D. 18..

....
[SEAL OF LODGE.] *Noble Grand.*

Such certificate shall be duly verified by the seal of the Lodge, and be transmitted to the Lodge before which the trial is pending.

In case there is no Lodge near the witness, the deposition may be taken by an officer authorized by the law of the State to administer oaths. The deposition of persons not members of the Order may be taken in evidence, the oath to be administered by an officer authorized by the law of the State to administer oaths. Depositions thus taken may be read in evidence in the cause to which they relate.

A case cannot be postponed to procure the testimony of an absent witness when the other party to the proceeding admits all that is assumed can be proved by such witness.

The accused, if he desire, shall be allowed to testify in his own behalf, the credibility of all witnesses being a matter for the consideration of the Trial Committee.

HOW CHARGES MAY BE PREFERRED AGAINST A MEMBER OF ANOTHER LODGE.

Charges may be preferred by a member of one Lodge against a member of another Lodge by presenting the charges to the Lodge of which the accuser is a member. Said Lodge shall forthwith forward to the Lodge to which the accused may belong a certified copy of the charges, over the signature of the Noble Grand and Secretary, and attested by the seal of the Lodge, and the Lodge to whom such charges shall be sent shall proceed to hear and determine the same in like manner as if preferred by a member of its own body. (Sec. 325, b. Digest S. G. L.)

Digest of Decisions

OF THE

R. W. GRAND LODGE OF NEVADA,

UP TO AND INCLUDING

THE SESSION OF 1881.

1. Actual service in office at least a majority of nights of a term (except when elected to fill a vacancy), is required to entitle an officer to the honors of the office, or the Past Official Degrees, and as thirteen nights do not constitute a majority of the term, officers are not entitled to the honors of the office. The rule applies to the officers of a new Lodge. (Vide Journal 1867, p. 58.)

2. It is not proper for a Lodge to pass a standing resolution granting the freedom of debate to a Brother of another jurisdiction upon all questions that may come before the Lodge. (Journal 1868, p. 149.)

3. The payment out of a Lodge fund for refreshments furnished on the occasion of installation of officers, is not one of the legitimate expenses of a Lodge, as recognized by authority, and consequently illegitimate. (Journal 1868, pp. 115, 140.)

4. D. D. Grand Masters are recommended to refrain from taking any active part in the business of their Lodges. (Journal 1868, pp. 118, 134.)

5. A Subordinate Lodge cannot exempt a new member from receiving benefits, unless he is disqualified by the By-laws. (Journal 1868, pp. 115, 134; Journal 1869, p. 236.)

7

6. A Lodge has full power to adopt and incorporate in its By-laws a form of prayer, to be used in opening and closing the Lodge. The Lodge has also full power to require a strict adherence to the form adopted, but cannot *oblige* any member of the Order to offer up his prayers to the Almighty in any form or language inconsistent with his religious belief; and it is not appropriate for the Chaplain of the Lodge to substitute his own form of prayer for that *adopted* by the Lodge, but he may decline to perform that particular duty at all. (Journal 1868, pp. 144, 150.)

7. If a Subordinate Lodge remits the dues of a member who has been suspended, but afterward refuses to reinstate him, the member is still a member suspended for non-payment of dues. (Journal 1868, pp. 153, 156.)

8. It is illegal to elect the Junior Past Grand to any elective office in his Lodge. (Journal 1869, pp. 196, 235.)

9. A Brother having committed suicide, and not being otherwise disqualified by the By-laws of his Lodge, or otherwise, is entitled to funeral benefits. (Journal 1869, pp. 196, 235.)

10. A visiting Brother of another jurisdiction must be examined as to his knowledge of the degree in which the Lodge is open, as well as in the A. T. P. W. (Journal 1869, pp. 196, 235.)

11. A visiting Brother of this jurisdiction holding a traveling card, in date, is entitled to the S. A. P. W., and the N. G. must invest him with the same on presentation of said card. (Journal 1869, pp. 196, 235.)

12. An expelled member of the Order cannot visit a Lodge, even should he be in possession of the S. A. P. W. for the term, and the N. G. would be right in refusing him admittance. (Journal 1869, pp. 196, 235.)

13. It is the duty of the N. G. to enforce the law as he finds and understands the same, subject to an appeal. (Journal 1867, pp. 196, 235.)

14. The Right Supporter of the N. G. occupies the N. G.'s chair temporarily, and may decide points of order. (Journal 1869, pp. 196, 235.)

15. The N. G. has a right to order a fine entered against a Brother for violation of any of the Rules of Order, without consulting the Lodge, subject always to an appeal thereto. (Journal 1869, pp. 196, 235.)

16. A motion of appeal from the decision of a Lodge does not cause a stay of proceedings until the appeal is decided. (Journal 1869, p. 243.)

17. A visiting Brother claiming to be a P. G., but whose card declares him only a Scarlet Degree member, cannot be admitted as a P. G., in the absence of members of the Lodge qualified to examine him as a P. G. (Journal 1869, p. 245.)

18. The act of a Lodge granting a Withdrawal Card severs a Brother's

connection with a Lodge, whether he takes a card or not. (Journal 1869, p. 245.)

19. The N. G., when occupying the chair, should put all questions himself, and not allow the V. G. to do so. (Journal 1869, p. 246.)

20. It is irregular for the R. W. Deputy Grand Master to issue a dispensation to a Lodge authorizing it to confer the three degrees upon Brothers who have been in membership only one week. (Journal 1869, p. 247.)

21. When a Brother signs the Constitution and By-laws of the Lodge, he then is admitted to full membership, which guarantees to him all the rights and privileges of an initiated member. (Journal 1868, pp. 133, 150.)

22. Any Brother eligible to the office of N. G., and who is duly elected as such to fill a vacancy, and is installed and serves as N. G. the remainder of the term, even if that is only one night, is entitled to all the honors of the office. (Journal 1868, p. 140.)

23. The law compelling Subordinate Lodges to pay the capitation tax before their officers are installed does not apply to the Degree of Daughter of Rebekah Lodges. The installing officer has no right to demand the tax, because Degree of Rebekah Lodges are Degree Lodges only and not Subordinate Lodges, in contemplation of Law. (Journal 1870, pp. 300, 354.)

24. It is legal to nominate and elect the same night an officer to fill a vacancy, when at a previous meeting all who had been nominated declined. (Journal 1870, pp. 300, 354.)

25. Although the By-laws of a Subordinate Lodge declare that blank ballots shall not be counted at an election for officers, yet the same being in contravention of the laws of the Sovereign Grand Lodge, I. O. O. F., the law is void, and blank ballots should legally be counted against a candidate. (Journal 1870, pp. 300, 332, 354.)

26. The proper practice would be to have the charges (against a Brother) and specifications in all cases entered upon the minutes of the Lodge. (Journal 1870, pp. 330, 352.)

27. A Brother filling an office to which there is attached an official degree, is entitled to receive said official degree even though he may receive a salary from the Lodge for his services—actual service in office the necessary number of nights being his passport to said official degree. (Journal 1871, pp. 380, 410, 425.)

28. A Subordinate Lodge can ask for relief only by consent of the Grand Lodge under which said Subordinate exists, and through the Grand Master of the jurisdiction to which the application for relief is made. (Journal 1871, pp. 380, 410, 425.)

29. It is proper to nominate and elect Brothers for officers of the Lodge during the absence of said Brothers, their consent being first gained. (Journal 1871, pp. 380, 410, 425.)

30. The true intent and meaning of Section 8 of Article V, of the Constitution of Subordinates, is to allow nominations for officers to be made both on the night the vacancy occurs and on the night of election. (Journal 1871, pp. 380, 410, 425.)

31. A Brother acting as Outside Guardian for several Lodges can only be installed into that office in the Lodge of which he is a member. (Journal 1871, pp. 381, 410, 425.)

32. A Lodge has a right to fine a Chaplain for absence when the By-laws so provide. (Journal 1871, pp. 381, 410, 425.)

33. A candidate for Noble Grand having been blanked, it is proper to open under the head of nominations for that office, provided there are no other members remaining in nomination for the office. (Journal 1871, pp. 381, 410, 425.)

34. All applicants for membership shall have actually resided in this jurisdiction for six months, and for thirty days next preceding his application in the city or town where the Lodge is located; and in case there is no Lodge in the city or town where the applicant resides, or in the county where he resides, then in the county nearest to where a Lodge is located. (Journal 1871, p. 419.)

35. It is necessary for the Recording Secretary to enter upon his minutes a synopsis only of all communications from all Grand Officers. (Journal 1872, p. 501.)

36. Rebekah Degree Lodges have a legal right to enact a By-law providing for a ballot on all applications for membership. (Journal 1872, pp. 501, 570.)

37. Past Grands can have no rights upon the floor of the Grand Lodge *as Representatives* from Lodges U. D. (Journal 1872, pp. 563, 569.)

38. A Lodge has no right to entertain charges against a Brother for debts on the outside of the Order. It has no right to interfere in the matter of a Brother's indebtedness with a member of the Order, or any one else. (Journal 1872, p. 580.)

39. A Brother must serve a majority of the nights of the term to entitle him to Past Official Degrees, and a resignation of the incumbent before the expiration of the term works a forfeiture of the right to obtain the said degrees. (Journal 1872, p. 584.)

40. The O. G., when called into the Lodge during the opening ceremony,

need not address the Chairs, but being required to enter the Lodge while it is working, he is subject to the same requirements in that particular as other officers or members. (Journal 1873, pp. 642, 726.)

41. The act of withdrawal from one Lodge and uniting with another in the same District does not work as a forfeiture of the office of District Deputy, providing membership be obtained in the second Lodge within thirty days; but no official act should be done while the Brother has no membership in either Lodge. (Journal 1873, pp. 642, 726.)

42. Under the provisions of Section 2 of Article XIII, of the Constitution of Subordinates, all amendments to the By-laws of a Lodge must be submitted through the Grand Secretary to the Committee on Laws of Subordinates, and be by them approved before going into effect. It matters not whether it be an entire new Code of By-laws or the changing of a single clause of a Section. (Journal 1873, pp. 642, 726.)

43. A V. G., elected and installed to fill a vacancy, may not appoint his Supporters, unless those appointed by his predecessor, and duly installed, shall first legally vacate their office. (Journal 1873, pp. 642, 726.)

44. Members of Sister Lodges may *not visit* on the P. W. of the term just expired, after the evening of installation of officers in the Lodge they propose to visit, even though the installation has not taken place in their own Lodge. (Journal 1873, pp. 642, 726.)

45. That the twenty-first standing resolution of this Grand Lodge is not to be construed as requiring the Secretaries and Treasurer of a Lodge to commit the initiatory and degree charges to memory to entitle them to installation, because it is not a part of their duties to confer any of said degrees. (Journal 1873, pp. 642, 726.)

46. If a card states that the holder thereof is a Past Grand, it is sufficient to entitle him to the privileges such rank confers, even though he be unable to prove himself in the work of that degree. But in case that evidence is omitted in the card and application be made to the Lodge issuing the card for a certificate in lieu thereof, "No ballot or vote should be taken upon granting a Past Grand's certificate after a faithful performance of the duties of the office of Noble Grand," says the Sovereign Grand Lodge. Hence held that it is the duty of the N. G. and Secretary to issue such certificate at once, in such cases, upon application. (Journal 1873, pp. 642, 726.)

47. A Lodge received a petition for initiation in which the name of the petitioner was so written that it was difficult to determine which of two certain names it was meant for. Three members entertaining some doubt as to the identity of the person voted unfavorably, rejecting the candidate. It subsequently appearing that the petitioner was every way worthy and that the Brothers voting unfavorably had been voting for the wrong name. *Held* that

no reconsideration was necessary, because they had not rejected the petitioner, not having voted for or against him at all, but for and against some one else, and having discovered their mistake it was proper for the N. G. to declare the ballot informal and void, and having caused his declaration entered on the records it was proper for him to order a ballot on the petition, the members being then for the first time able to vote intelligently. (Journal 1873, pp. 643, 726.)

48. A Past Grand is eligible to election as a Representative to this Grand Lodge, notwithstanding the fact that he is serving his Lodge as N. G. and will still be so serving at the time of the annual session. (Journal 1873, pp. 643, 726.)

49. A Subordinate Lodge working under Dispensation or Warrant is not entitled to representation in the Grand Lodge. But there is no reason why it may not elect three representatives for its charter, to take their seats as soon as the charter is granted. (Journal 1873, pp. 643, 726.)

50. All names reported in the Grand Secretary's quarterly circular or " Black List " must be entered or "posted " in the " Black Book " of each Lodge, except those already entered or posted, upon information received from sister Lodges in the same District. (Journal 1873, pp. 644, 726.)

51. If a Noble Grand tender his resignation and it be accepted by the Lodge, his duties as such officer immediately cease, and it is the duty of the V. G. to at once assume the chair and appoint some qualified Brother to perform the duties of Vice Grand. (Journal 1873, pp. 701, 726.)

52. The funeral regalia of the Order only shall be worn at funerals, except by permission of the Grand Master. (Journal 1873, pp. 720, 732.)

53. The V. G. must read the obligation from the book and not deliver the same from memory. (Journal 1874, pp. 779, 854.)

54. An application for a " Withdrawal Card " can only be made by the Brother in person in open Lodge, or by a written request over his own signature, or by a Brother of the Order in good standing, who may have received authority from the Brother to make the application for him, or by a person not a member of the Order, who may exhibit an application for the same on the Brother's signature. (Journal 1874, pp. 779, 854.)

55. A Card after being granted should not be delivered to a person not a member of the Order. (Journal 1874, pp. 780, 854.)

56. It is not proper for a Conductor during an initiation to wear Helmet, Shield and Sword. (Journal 1874, pp. 780, 854.)

57. It is not proper to admit a Brother during the initiation of a Candidate, and the Initiation is only complete after the Candidate has been introduced to the Lodge. (Journal 1874, pp. 780, 854.)

58. Twenty-six nights service in some inferior office other than that of Permanent Secretary or Chaplain, is requisite to entitle a Brother to be eligible for the office of V. G. (Journal 1874, pp. 780, 854.)

59. A Lodge cannot grant leave of absence to an officer who has not served a majority of nights of the term to enable him to receive the past Official Degrees. (Journal 1874, pp. 780, 854.)

60. A Brother holding the office of D. D. G. M. is not eligible to the office of Secretary of his Lodge. (Journal 1875, pp. 917, 1008.)

61. That a miscount of votes does not affect the right of a Brother to be installed N. G. of his Lodge, who received a majority of the votes cast. (Journal 1875, pp. 917, 1008.)

62. A new ballot is proper when a discrepancy appears between the number of ballots announced by the tellers and the number shown by the canvass. (Journal 1875, pp. 917, 1008.)

63. That it was improper to admit members into Genoa Lodge, No. 15, who were residents of the jurisdiction of California, other than those who were residents of Alpine and Mono counties. (Journal 1875, pp. 917, 1008.)

64. Representatives to this Grand Lodge are not legally elected unless such election is held at a regular meeting of the Subordinate. (Journal 1875, pp. 917, 1008.)

65. The election of a Representative who is not in good standing at the time of such election is illegal. (Journal 1875, pp. 917, 1008.)

66. It is illegal to grant a certificate to a Representative who was elected at a special meeting called by the N. G., or who was not in good standing at the time of his election. (Journal 1875, pp. 917, 1008.)

67. That the right to ballot for the admission of a member carries with it the implied right to ballot upon any penalty, and that it is not only the right but the duty of the N. G. to vote upon the determination of the penalty, and that no law or rule of order of a Subordinate Lodge can deprive him of that privilege. (Journal 1875, pp. 990, 999.)

68. A Brother holding a card out of date may be admitted into a procession by the consent of the Lodge forming such procession. (Journal 1875, pp. 1007, 1008.)

69. A non-affiliate, a suspended or expelled Odd Fellow has no right to appear in procession in regalia. (Journal 1875, pp. 1007, 1008.)

70. A nominee who has been beaten by blank ballots, and declared out of nomination by the N. G., can be renominated for the same office at the same election. (Journal 1875, pp 1007, 1008.)

71. The Grand Master and his District Deputies have the right to grant dispensations for Lodges to turn out in regalia at funerals, upon proper application by any Lodge within this jurisdiction. (Journal 1875, pp. 989, 1013.)

72. A Committee on Investigation has a right to inquire, in writing or verbally, of another Lodge in this jurisdiction as to the character of an applicant for membership. (Journal 1875, p. 983.)

73. Subordinate Lodges have the exclusive control of their own funds with regard to benefits, as well as other matters, subject only to the laws of the Sovereign Grand Lodge and the laws of this Grand Lodge, and that this Grand Lodge should not interfere with this prerogative. (Journal 1875, pp. 989, 990.)

74. A Lodge can, by permission of the Grand Lodge, hold sessions less often than once a week; but, when they do so, their officers must hold their offices one year. (Journal 1875, pp. 1007, 1008.)

75. It is necessary for a Brother to pay his dues during the entire time o his suspension, he having been suspended for conduct unbecoming an Odd Fellow. (Journal 1876, p. 1090.)

76. A Lodge cannot open for the transaction of business a quorum of members being present, but the N. G. and V. G. being absent and no P. G. present. (Journal 1876, p. 1099.)

77. A Brother, being on the sick list, removes to a place where no Lodge exists, and has to furnish, when demanded, a certificate from a physician or a magistrate. A certificate from a person who is not actually practicing his profession, but merely states that at some prior time he has practiced, cannot be accredited by a Lodge. (Journal 1876, p. 1099.)

78. That property acquired by a Lodge is its own, subject to the rights of the Grand Lodge upon the surrender of its Charter.

That the Lodge has the right, in the exercise of a sound discretion and for the good of the Order, to sell any of the property of the Lodge.

That, as to a library of a Lodge, the Lodge has a right to say who shall be the custodian of their library and where it shall be kept. It has a right to rent a library, as well as a Lodge-room. It therefore follows that a Lodge has the right, within the full sense of the words, " to sell " or " lend " its library, or any part thereof, but cannot give it away.

That it makes no difference in this matter how the library was acquired by the Lodge. (Journal 1876, pp. 1106, 1121.)

79. It is a settled law in this jurisdiction that a reconsideration of a vote by which Representatives to the Grand Lodge are elected is out of Order, and cannot be entertained. (See Journal 1876, p. 1115.)

80. A Brother having been declared in contempt by a Trial Committee,

the N. G. should declare the Brother expelled, without a ballot of the Lodge ; contempt being an offense with a specific penalty provided by the Constitution of Subordinates. (Secs. 5 and 6, Art. VII. Journal 1877, pp. 1159, 1192, 1193, 1200.)

81. Section 940, White's Digest, does not apply to Trustees of a Lodge ; they not being officers in the meaning of that section. (Journal 1877, pp. 1159, 1160, 1192, 1193, 1200.)

82. It is competent for a Lodge to re-elect its N. G., there being no law to the contrary. (Journal 1877, pp. 1159, 1192, 1193, 1200.)

83. A man cannot become an Odd Fellow who cannot read and write. (Journal 1877, pp. 1159, 1192, 1193, 1200.)

84. Officers of a new Lodge being instituted but two months are not entitled to the honors, and would hold over until the expiration of the next term, when their successors should be elected. (See White's Digest, p. 330, Sections 1552, 1553. Journal 1878, pp. 1254, 1291, 1319.)

85. The Noble Grand of a Lodge has no right to wear a collar with gold links and yellow metal fringe while acting as N. G. The law prescribes his regalia, and the Lodge has no right to have that officer's regalia trimmed in that manner. (Journal 1878, pp. 1254, 1291, 1319.)

86. The Vice Grand of a Lodge, after having the door placed in his charge by the N. G., has a right to admit members of his own Lodge without the pass-word; he (the V. G.) knowing that they have not been suspended for non-payment of dues. (Journal 1878, pp. 1254, 1291, 1319.)

87. A proposition for membership may be withdrawn at any time before the report of the committee thereon is read in the Lodge, but not afterwards. (Journal 1878, pp. 1254, 1291, 1319.)

88. A Brother who was suspended for a definite time must pay his dues during suspension. The suspension being inflicted as a punishment, deprives him of all benefits, but does not relieve him of his obligation to his Lodge during that time. (Journal 1878, pp. 1254, 1291, 1319.)

89. A Brother suspended for cause must pay the amount of dues legally accrued against him on the books of the Lodge up to the date of reinstatement. It is the duty of the Secretary to notify the Brother, while under suspension, that he is twelve months in arrears; and of the Lodge to read him out, provided the requirements of the Constitution of Subordinates have been complied with. (Journal 1878, pp. 1307, 1315, 1324.)

90. It is improper and illegal for the N. G. and V. G., or N. G. and V. G. elect of any Subordinate Lodge in this jurisdiction to receive any instruction in the secret work of the Order, except from the M. W. Grand Master and the proper officers, the requirements of the Constitution of Subordinates having been complied with. (Journal 1877, pp. 1307, 1315, 1324.)

Deputy Grand Master or District Deputies throughout this jurisdiction. (Journal 1879, pp. 1398, 1406)

91. It is the duty of every District Deputy Grand Master appointed by the M. W. Grand Master to make a full and complete report of his work and the condition of the Lodges under his control to the M. W. Grand Master at least ten days prior to the meeting of the R. W. Grand Lodge in each year. (Journal 1879, pp. 1398, 1406.)

92. Where charges have been preferred, investigated and dismissed, it is illegal to re-prefer the same charges against a Brother. (Journal 1879, pp. 1393, 1406.)

93. Where penalties have been legally prescribed by Subordinate Lodges the Grand Lodge will not interfere. (Journal 1879, pp. 1395, 1406.)

94. Members of the Rebekah Degree not members of a regularly chartered Rebekah Degree Lodge, are not entitled to visit a regularly chartered Rebekah Degree Lodge. The S. A. P. W. being given to the officers of such Lodges only, the Grand Master has no right to introduce such members of this degree. (Journal 1880, pp. 13, 57, 59.)

95. *Question*—Can a Lodge, by resolution, declare a member expelled from the Order who is in State Prison for the crime of embezzlement, he having acknowledged his guilt as charged ?

Answer—No. By referring to Article VII, Section 4, of the Constitution, and page 43 of the Code of Procedure, you will find that charges must be preferred. (Journal 1881, pp. 123, 191, 196.)

96. That no one is eligible to membership in a Rebekah Degree Lodge, nor can make application for membership, until he or she has first received the Degree of Rebekah. (Journal 1881, pp. 123, 192, 196.)

97. That no wife, sister or daughter of any Scarlet Degree member can receive the Degree of Rebekah, unless such member shall have first applied for it, and received the consent of the Subordinate Lodge of which he is a member. (Journal 1881, pp. 123, 192, 196.)

98. That such degree having been applied for by a husband, father or brother who is a Scarlet Degree member in good standing, the degree must be conferred on the one for whom the application is made, without the ordeal of a ballot. (Journal 1881, pp. 123, 192, 196.)

99. That it is the duty of a Subordinate Lodge to confer the degree, or it can ask a Rebekah Lodge to do it. But the fact of a Rebekah Degree Lodge existing in the town or place would not deprive a Subordinate Lodge of the right to confer it, should circumstances ever make such a course advisable. (Journal 1881, pp. 123, 192, 196.)

100. That the conferring of the Rebekah Degree upon a wife, sister or brother, by a Rebekah Degree Lodge, does not make such wife, sister or brother a member of such Lodge; but after such degree is conferred, he or she must retire and apply for membership in usual form, and undergo an investigation and ballot. (Journal 1881, pp. 123, 192, 196.)

101. That the first resolution on pages 8089 and 8176—Sovereign Grand Lodge, 1879—empowers Subordinate Lodges, as well as Rebekah Degree Lodges to confer the Rebekah Degree on any unmarried sister or daughter over eighteen years of age of any Scarlet Degree member in good standing who makes application for such, as well as on his wife. (Journal 1881, pp. 123, 124, 192, 196.)

102. All rejections—whether by deposit of card, as Ancient Odd Fellow, or non-affiliate—must be reported, the same as an application by initiation. (Journal 1881, pp. 124, 192, 196.)

103. A sister of a Third Degree member in good standing, who, at the time of application, is a divorced woman, is entitled to receive the Degree of Rebekah. (Journal 1881, pp. 124, 192, 196; also, see Sovereign Grand Lodge Proceedings of 1880, p. 8211.)

104. A member is not eligible for V. G., unless he has served a majority of the nights of a term in an inferior office, and that such service must be *actual* and not *constructive*, and that the fact of the officer being excused from time to time for non-attendance, does not absolve him from the requirements of the law governing the qualifications of officers. (Journal 1881, pp. 124, 125, 192, 196.)

105. The Deputy Grand Master, or any other elective officer of the Grand Lodge, is entitled to the honors of the Order, when he announces himself officially for the purpose of introducing a visiting Brother. (Journal 1881, pp. 124, 192, 196.)

106. A Lodge has control over its funds with regard to benefits or relief, subject only to the laws of the Sovereign Grand Lodge, and this Grand Lodge, and there is no law governing the amount of donations.

That Subordinate Lodges have the right to determine the propriety of appropriating their funds for all purposes recognized by the Order. (Digest, 550. Journal 1881, pp. 167, 168, 192, 193, 196.)

107. This Grand Lodge has repeatedly affirmed that it will not disturb the penalty imposed by a Subordinate Lodge, when the same has been legally prescribed. That when the judgment of a Lodge is sustained by the testimony, and in compliance with the laws of the Order, it *will not* interfere. (Journal 1881, pp. 170, 171, 183.)

108. An appeal from the decision of the D. D. Grand Master on a "ques-

tion of law" should be taken to the M. W. Grand Master. (Journal 1881, pp. 172, 183.)

109. A Brother who is over thirteen weeks in arrears, and is taken sick while in arrears, cannot pay his dues and reinstate himself so as to be entitled to benefits during that sickness. (Journal 1881, p. 199.)

110. A Brother has a right to decline a nomination for an elective office at any time after being nominated; *provided*, the By laws of the Lodge do not prescribe to the contrary. (Journal 1881, pp. 193, 200.)

STANDING RESOLUTIONS

OF THE

STANDING RESOLUTIONS

OF THE

R. W. GRAND LODGE OF NEVADA,

UP- TO AND. INCLUDING

THE SESSION OF 1881.

1. That all resolutions offered in this Grand Lodge shall be presented in duplicate ; shall be on paper equal in size at least to half a page of foolscap, and shall be accompanied by the name of the Representative proposing the same. (Journal 1867, p. 46.)

2. That the Grand Secretary be authorized to retain at all times in his hands the sum of seventy-five dollars out of moneys received by him, for the renewal of supplies and the payment of the incidental expenses of his office ; and he shall keep and present at each Annual Communication an accurate account of moneys expended for such supplies and incidental expenses. (Journal 1867, p. 47.)

3. That the Grand Secretary is hereby instructed to transmit to the Subordinate Lodges, quarterly, on the first of January, April, July and October of each year, a list of rejections, suspensions, ceased membership and reinstatements in Subordinate Lodges, and that he have prepared and forward to Subordinate Lodges proper blanks for their semi-annual returns. (Journal 1867, p. 57.)

4. That drunkenness and gambling are in open violation against the principles of Odd Fellowship, and the Brother who shall have been found guilty of

either of these vices may be suspended or expelled from his Lodge. (Journal 1868, p. 135.)

5. That the R. W. Grand Secretary be instructed to transmit to each Subordinate Lodge in this jurisdiction, on or before the first of April in each year, notification of the number of Representatives to which such Lodge will be entitled at the next ensuing Annual Session of the Grand Lodge, computed on the basis of the semi-annual report of such Lodge, for the term ending on the 31st day of December previous thereto ; and that, at the same time, the Grand Secretary shall furnish each Subordinate Lodge with a sufficient number of printed blank credentials for Representatives and Past Grands. (Journal 1868, p. 154.)

6. That when Lodges purchase new Charge Books, and place the old ones in the hands of the District Deputy Grand Master, as at present required, that officer shall forthwith burn said old books, and immediately make report of the fact to the Grand Secretary. (Journal 1869, p. 236.)

7. That upon the death, resignation or removal from office of the Recording Secretary of a Subordinate Lodge, the N. G. of the Lodge shall, under seal of the Lodge, immediately notify the Grand Secretary thereof; and in like manner shall notify the Grand Secretary of the election and installation to fill the vacancy. (Journal 1869, p. 236.)

8. That it is an inherent and individual right which each Brother should be allowed to exercise in voting for officers in Subordinate Lodges, to cast his own ballot, and should he desire to cast a blank one, to do so. It is therefore illegal to instruct the Secretary or other officer or member of the Lodge to cast the ballot of the Lodge, even should there be but one candidate in nomination; but each Brother shall declare his choice by casting his own ballot. (Journal 1869, p. 237.)

9. That a Secretary has no right to read, or Lodge to entertain, an anonymous communication. (Journal 1869, p. 243.)

10. That no member of the Committee on Appeals shall act as an attorney or counselor for another in any trial or proceedings in the Grand or Subordinate Lodges; to take effect from and after this session of the Grand Lodge. (Journal 1870, p. 338.)

11. That all reports submitted by committees, except those made on the last day of the session, shall, after being read to the Grand Lodge, lie on the table until the following day. (Journal 1870, p. 338.)

12. That in the election of two Grand Representatives the Brother receiving the largest majority vote shall be declared elected for two years, and the Brother receiving the next largest majority vote shall be declared elected for one year. (Journal 1870, p. 339.)

13. That the Grand Secretary be, and he is hereby, instructed to prepare,

at each Annual Communication of this R. W. Grand Lodge, and publish with the proceedings thereof, a table showing what Representatives are present, as well as those absent, at each day's session. (Journal 1871, p. 368.)

14. That at all regular and special meetings of this Grand Lodge all officers or committeemen previously elected or appointed, whether returned to this Grand Lodge as Representatives at the next session after their election or appointment, or not, shall have the right to make such reports of their work as they may deem proper, and this R. W. Grand Lodge shall hear and entertain such reports. (Journal 1871, p. 408.)

15. That the Recording Secretaries of Subordinate Lodges be, and they are hereby, required to indorse on the back of visiting cards presented by visiting members any and all sums of money that may be donated by ·their Lodge for the pecuniary assistance of such visiting member. (Journal 1871, pp. 410, 425.)

16. That it is proper to elect Brothers for officers of the Lodge during the absence of said Brothers, their consent being first given. (Journal 1871, p. 428.)

17. That the indefinite postponement of any question under consideration in a Subordinate Lodge disposes of said question for the term. (Journal 1871, p. 429.)

18. That, hereafter, the Representatives from the Districts in this jurisdiction hand in the names of those whom they wish to have appointed as District Deputies on the first day of the session of this Grand Lodge. That on the first day of the sessions of this Grand Lodge, hereafter, the M. W. Grand Master shall appoint a committee of three to examine those whose names are presented for District Deputies. That the said committee shall report on the third day of the session the names of those whom the committee find qualified for the appointment of District Deputies. (Journal 1871, p. 432.)

19. All questions of usage and law propounded to the Grand Lodge shall be referred to the proper committee, without being entered upon the Journal, unless otherwise ordered by the Grand Lodge. (Journal 1872.)

20. All proposed amendments to the Constitution of this Grand Lodge, or of its Subordinates, shall contain the section or sections written out in full, as proposed to be amended. (Journal 1872.)

21. All District Deputy Grand Masters or installing officers in this jurisdiction are instructed to fully examine each elective officer in their respective Districts relative to his proficiency in the work of the Order, and to install no such officer unless he has the charges and work of his office fully committed to memory; *provided*, that this shall not be so construed as to prevent the installation of the first officers of a new Lodge. (Journal 1872.) ·

22. A Subordinate Lodge may legitimately appropriate money from its funds to defray the expenses of its Representatives to the Grand Lodge. (Journal 1872.)

23. A Lodge has power to donate money to put into good standing a member who is afflicted with sickness or disability to follow his usual occupation. (Journal 1872.) *A Lodge may legitimately appropriate money from its funds . . .*

24. Subordinate Lodges must transmit to the Grand Secretary, in all appeal cases, the *full* proceedings had in such cases, of whatever nature, and cannot refuse to allow appeals; or to transmit copies of any papers the appellant deems necessary; *provided*, notice of appeal be given within the time required by the Constitution. (Journal 1872.)

25. Secretaries of all Lodges in this jurisdiction are required to furnish to the Grand Secretary of this Grand Lodge a certificate, under seal, containing a list of Representatives elect, and of Past Grands in good standing, at least one week prior to the session of the Grand Lodge in each year. (Journal 1872.)

26. That a sum equal to the traveling expenses of one Representative from each Lodge to the R. W. Grand Lodge, and return, be paid out of the funds of this R. W. Grand Lodge, to the Representative, or Representatives proportionately, in attendance at the annual session thereof. (Journal 1872, p. 549.)

27. That the R. W. Grand Secretary be, and he is hereby authorized, to draw his warrant upon the R. W. Grand Treasurer, from time to time, in favor of the M. W. Grand Master for his traveling expenses in visiting officially the different Lodges within this jurisdiction, not to exceed the sum of $500 annually. (Journal 1872.)

28. That it is hereby made the duty of the Recording Secretaries of the several Subordinate Lodges under the jurisdiction of this Grand Lodge, upon the death of any Past Noble Grand in membership in their Lodge, to forthwith report to the R. W. Grand Secretary the date of death, together with the name of the deceased, and such other facts relating to the past services of the deceased in Odd Fellowship as may come to their knowledge. (Journal 1872.)

29. That at this, and all subsequent Annual Sessions, the R. W. Grand Secretary be and he is hereby authorized to draw his warrant on the Grand Treasurer for a sum, not to exceed the sum of $35, for the purpose of procuring the P. G. Master's photograph, immediately after the adjournment of the Grand Lodge. (Journal 1872.)

30. That the Grand Secretary be, and is hereby authorized to procure a sufficient supply of the new edition of the Digest of the Sovereign Grand Lodge

for the use of the Order in this State, to be sold by him as other supplies. (Journal 1872.)

31. That the Representatives who shall from time to time be accredited to this Grand Lodge be requested to carefully collect and present to this Grand Lodge such facts and incidents as they may be able to obtain concerning deceased members of this Grand Lodge. (Journal 1873, p. 707.)

32. That the P. W. be changed semi-annually. (Journal 1873, pp. 719, 732.)

33. That the Grand Master be empowered and is hereby authorized to create, during recess, new districts and change old ones, subject to the approval of the Grand Lodge at the next ensuing session. (Journal 1873, pp. 719, 732.)

34. That Representatives to this Grand Lodge who do not appear and report to this Grand Body on the first day of the session, or leave without permission of this Grand Lodge during the session, are not entitled to traveling expenses as authorized by Standing Resolution No. 26. (Journal 1875, pp. 994, 995.)

35. That in the election of Representatives to this R. W. Grand Lodge by Subordinate Lodges each Past Grand nominated shall pledge himself, or some member of the Lodge in good standing for him, that he will, if elected, attend the session of the R. W. Grand Lodge and perform the duty required of him, unless prevented by sickness or other unavoidable accident, in which case they will inform the Lodge of that fact, and the Lodge shall proceed to elect Representatives to fill vacancies thus occasioned and the Secretary shall notify the Grand Secretary of any and all such changes made. (Journal 1875, pp 1004, 1005.)

36. That the Grand Secretary be, and is hereby, required, upon the institution of any new Lodge within this jurisdiction, to notify all other Lodges in said jurisdiction of the institution of said new Lodge. (Journal 1875, p. 979.)

37. That no resolution having in view the amending of any fundamental law of this R. W. Grand Lodge be entertained, except it be offered on the first day's meeting of this R. W. Grand Lodge. (Journal 1876, p. 1122.)

38. That each Subordinate Lodge in this jurisdiction shall obtain and keep in the archives of the Lodge, for the purpose of reference, a copy of the History and Code of Procedure in trials adopted by this Grand Lodge, and the Digest of the Sovereign Grand Lodge. (Journal 1876, p. 1123.)

39. That the Chairman of the Committee on Appeals be entitled to one bound copy of the Proceedings of this Grand Lodge, the same to be returned to this Lodge. (Journal 1876, p. 1128.)

40. That the Executive Committee be authorized and directed hereafter
9

to publish such Grand Officers' reports as may be transmitted to the Grand Secretary before the convening of this Grand Lodge. (Journal 1877, p. 1188.)

41. That it shall be the duty of the R. W. Grand Secretary of the R. W. Grand Lodge of Nevada, immediately after the close of each annual session of this Grand Body, to transmit under the seal of this Grand Lodge a "remittitur" to the Lodge so appealing, etc., showing in brief terms the action of this Grand Body upon any case which may have been appealed to this R. W. Grand Lodge or any question which may have been submitted to this Grand Body for decision from any Subordinate Lodge in this jurisdiction. (Journal 1879, p. 1423.)

42. That the custom heretofore had in delaying the getting out of the printed Journal until after the reports from the Subordinates for the present term are received by the Grand Secretary be rescinded, and the Grand Secretary be instructed to make up and have printed the Journal of the session as soon after adjournment as practicable. (Journal 1879, p. 1420.)

43. That the Trustees of this R. W. Grand Lodge be, and they are hereby, required to report to this Grand Lodge at each annual session the amount, value, character and condition of all the property belonging to this Grand Lodge. (Journal 1880, p. 64.)

44. That the sum of $60 be and is hereby appropriated out of the funds of this R. W. Grand Lodge for the purpose of procuring a jewel for the retiring Grand Master, and the R. W. G. Secretary be authorized to draw his warrant for the amount. (Journal 1880, p. 71.)

45. Inasmuch as the Grand Secretary's financial report is a complete account of the receipts and expenditures of this Grand Body,

Resolved, That hereafter it be printed in full in the Journal of Proceedings, and that a synopsis only of the Grand Treasurer's report be printed. (Journal 1881, pp. 173, 183.)

46. It is recommended that the minute books of the Lodges be kept with a marginal index on the pages; also, that a press letter book be kept, in which shall be copied all the correspondence of the Lodge, all notices to delinquent members, and all other papers of which it is necessary to keep copies. (Journal 1881, pp. 175, 179.)

47. That the N. G. of a Subordinate Lodge, or the Brother filling said position, upon leaving his chair for the purpose of taking part in debate on any question, shall not return to his seat during the pendency of said question. (Journal 1881, p. 198.)

48. That the R. W. Grand Secretary be, and he is hereby instructed, to remove the photograph of any Past Grand Master from his office, when he

receives notice from a Subordinate Lodge that said P. G. M. has ceased membership for non-payment of dues. (Journal 1881, p. 198.)

49. That hereafter all salaries and appropriations to officers of this R. W. Grand Lodge be fixed prior to the election of such officers for the ensuing year. (Journal 1881, p. 206.)

OFFICE OF GRAND SECRETARY

OF THE

R. W. GRAND LODGE, I. O. O. F.,

OF THE

STATE OF NEVADA,

VIRGINIA, NEV., July 1st, 1881.

I hereby certify that the foregoing, comprising:

1st. Constitution of the Grand Lodge and Rules of Order,

2d. Constitution of Subordinate Lodges,

3d. Constitution of Rebekah Degree Lodges,

4th. The Code of Procedure regulating Trials and Appeals,

5th. A Digest of all Decisions of the Grand Lodge,

6th. All Standing Resolutions of the Grand Lodge,

Are correct in all particulars, as revised and amended at the Fifteenth Annual Communication of the R. W. Grand Lodge in 1881.

ATTEST:

WM. H. HILL,

Grand Secretary.

INDEX.

Constitution of Grand Lodge.

Constitution of Subordinates.

Constitution of Rebekah Degree Lodges.

Code of Procedure.

Index to Decisions and Standing Resolutions.

DECISIONS.

STANDING RESOLUTIONS.

ERRATA. — On page 40, "TRIAL COMMITTEE," should read: "The Trial Committee shall be appointed as provided by Section 10, Article V, Constitution of Subordinates, and shall consist of five members, who must be, if possible, the peers of the accused.

www.ingramcontent.com/pod-product-compliance
Lightning Source LLC
Chambersburg PA
CBHW020230090426
42735CB00010B/1632